Calgary's Best Hikes and Walks

Lori Beattie

FIFTH
HOUSE

Fifth House Ltd. acknowledges with thanks The Canada Council for the Arts and Ontario
Arts Council for their support of our publishing program. We also acknowledge the financial support of the Government of Canada through the Canada Book Fund.

 Canada Council **Conseil des Arts**
for the Arts **du Canada**

 ONTARIO ARTS COUNCIL
CONSEIL DES ARTS DE L'ONTARIO

Printed in Canada

06 / 2007

National Library of Canada Cataloguing in Publication Data
Beattie, Lori.
    Calgary's best hikes and walks
ISBN 978-1-894004-73-2
1. Hiking—Alberta—Calgary—Guidebooks. 2. Walking—Alberta—Calgary—
Guidebooks. 3. Calgary (Alta.)—Guidebooks. I. Title.
GV199.44.C22C33 2002   917.123'38043   C2001-911705-1

Fifth House Ltd.
A Fitzhenry & Whiteside Company
195 Allstate Parkway,
Markham, ON, L3S 4H2
1-800-387-9776
www.fifthhousepublishers.ca

Fitzhenry & Whiteside Ltd.
311 Washington Street,
Brighton, Massachusetts, 02135

 MIX
Paper from
responsible sources
FSC® C016245

Table of Contents

Legend   viii

Location Map   ix

Acknowledgements   x

Chapter 1: Introduction   1

Chapter 2: Trail Training   3

    Aerobic and Anaerobic Exercise   3

    Three Steps to a Successful and Enjoyable
    Outdoor Fitness Experience   4

    Training Tips for Neophyte Hikers and
    Hard-Core Backpackers   6

Chapter 3: Clothing, Gear, and Food
  for Outdoor Activity   13

    Fueling Up   13

    Layers   14

    Socks   16

    Footwear   16

    Backpacks   17

    Hiking Poles   17

Chapter 4: The Hikes   19

    Categories   20

    Degree of Difficulty   21

    Trail Etiquette and Safety   22

Hike 1: Twelve Mile Coulee, NW   23

Hike 2: Edgemont Park Ravine, NW   26

Hike 3: Edgemont Hills, NW   30

Hike 4: West Nose Creek Park, NE   34

Nose Hill Park: An Overview   38

Hike 5: Porcupine Valley (Nose Hill), NW   40

Hike 6: Rubbing Stone Hill (Nose Hill), NW   44

Hike 7: Many Owls Valley (Nose Hill), NW   48

Hike 8: Bowmont Park West, NW   52

Hike 9: Bowmont Park East, NW   56

Hike 10: Bowness Park/Bow River, NW   59

Hike 11: Bowness/Shouldice Park, NW   62

Hike 12: Confederation Park/Nose Hill, NW   65

Hike 13: Briar Hill/Parkdale, NW   69

Hike 14: McHugh Bluff/Prince's Island, NW   72

Hike 15: Regal Terrace/Sunnyside, NE/NW   76

Hike 16: Bridgeland/Bow River, NE   80

Hike 17: Strathcona Ravine, SW   83

Hike 18: Edworthy Park, SW   85

Hike 19: Douglas Fir Trail, SW   88

Hike 20: Bow River/Scarboro, SW   92

Hike 21: Elbow Park/Mount Royal, SW   95

Hike 22: Ramsay/Inglewood, SE   98

Hike 23: Inglewood Bird Sanctuary, SE   102

Hike 24: Roxboro/Stanley Park, SW   105

Hike 25: Reader Rock Garden/Elbow River, SW   108

Hike 26: Garrison Woods/Marda Loop, SW   112

Hike 27: Glenmore Dam/Bel-Aire, SW   117

Hike 28: Sandy Beach/Mount Royal, SW   121

Hike 29: Britannia/Parkhill, SW   124

Hike 30: Beaverdam Flats Park/Carburn Park, SE   127

Hike 31: Weaselhead Flats/North Glenmore Park, SW   130

Hike 32: North Glenmore Park/Lakeview, SW   134

Hike 33: Jackrabbit Trail, SW   137

Fish Creek Provincial Park: An Overview   140

Hike 34: Ridgeview Trail (Fish Creek), SW   142

Hike 35: Raven Rocks (Fish Creek), SW   147

Hike 36: Bow Valley Ranch (Fish Creek), SE   150

Hike 37: Mallard Point (Fish Creek), SE   156

Appendix: The Best of Calgary's Best Hikes and Walks   158

Index   163

Legend

ROUTE PATHWAY

paved road	paved path	unpaved path	grass path

NEARBY PATHWAYS

paved road	paved path	unpaved path	grass path

route continuance between map plates

parking		fence	
restroom	*R*	powerline	
hike start	**X**	picnic area	
foot bridge		playgound	
traffic bridge	) (	on-leash area	
stairs		off-leash area	
interpretive sign		coffee shop	
other sign		landmark building	
viewpoint		school	
LRT station		church	
LRT		house	
railroad		downslope	

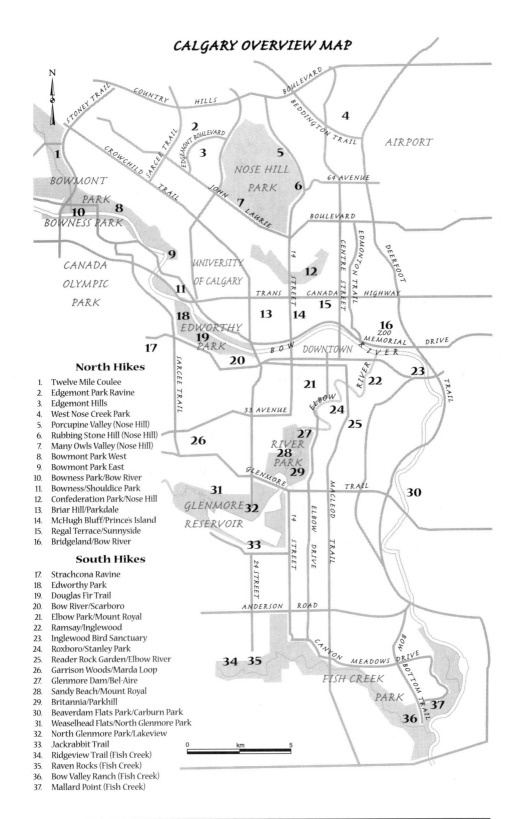

CALGARY OVERVIEW MAP

North Hikes

1. Twelve Mile Coulee
2. Edgemont Park Ravine
3. Edgemont Hills
4. West Nose Creek Park
5. Porcupine Valley (Nose Hill)
6. Rubbing Stone Hill (Nose Hill)
7. Many Owls Valley (Nose Hill)
8. Bowmont Park West
9. Bowmont Park East
10. Bowness Park/Bow River
11. Bowness/Shouldice Park
12. Confederation Park/Nose Hill
13. Briar Hill/Parkdale
14. McHugh Bluff/Prince's Island
15. Regal Terrace/Sunnyside
16. Bridgeland/Bow River

South Hikes

17. Strachcona Ravine
18. Edworthy Park
19. Douglas Fir Trail
20. Bow River/Scarboro
21. Elbow Park/Mount Royal
22. Ramsay/Inglewood
23. Inglewood Bird Sanctuary
24. Roxboro/Stanley Park
25. Reader Rock Garden/Elbow River
26. Garrison Woods/Marda Loop
27. Glenmore Dam/Bel-Aire
28. Sandy Beach/Mount Royal
29. Britannia/Parkhill
30. Beaverdam Flats Park/Carburn Park
31. Weaselhead Flats/North Glenmore Park
32. North Glenmore Park/Lakeview
33. Jackrabbit Trail
34. Ridgeview Trail (Fish Creek)
35. Raven Rocks (Fish Creek)
36. Bow Valley Ranch (Fish Creek)
37. Mallard Point (Fish Creek)

Acknowledgements

Many thanks to the Fit Frogs! Over the past five years my hiking clients have tested every inch of the routes provided in this book. Always upbeat and positive, they have fun climbing hills (even the 4th and 5th time), enjoy curb-side stretches (even when cab-drivers stop to ask "is this some kind of winter yoga?") and are a heck of a lot of fun to be around! Here's to more hikes with the Fit Frogs!

Thanks so much to my friends Carmen and Randall Berlin who took to the trails to test every one of the hikes in this book. The time and expertise of friends Tammy Lee and Charlene Owen made the stretching photos look great.

An exceptional person played a major role in the creation of my company and, in a round-about way, the writing of this book. Before his untimely death in 1998, Gary Coulman was a hiker extraordinaire with a great sense of humour and wit. He was my ultimate supporter and a true friend.

I appreciate the attention to detail and the enthusiasm of Charlene Dobmeier and Richard Janzen at Fifth House Publishers and the graphic design work done by Mike and Brian at Articulate Eye Design.

Thanks to Margaret and Donald Beattie who get excited about all my projects. And the biggest thanks goes to Keith Dewing, the most wonderful person I have ever met!

1

Introduction

Explore Calgary on foot! The maze of urban pathways in this guidebook takes you on walking adventures in the heart of Calgary. No fancy gear is needed, just an eagerness to savour the city's best trails, parks, and neighbourhoods.

The treks described here are perfect for everyone with a hectic schedule. When you do not have a full day available to head to the mountains, make time for a short urban hike in the evening. Invite a friend along for a hike and brunch on a crisp winter morning. Sunshine, fresh air, and friendly chatter, followed by hot chocolate and a ginger scone, are sure to lift your spirits during the dark months. Slow your city pace and follow trails that lead you over hill and down dale, through neighbourhoods and parks, and past playgrounds, coffee shops, and Christmas-light displays.

The hikes in this book are as varied as the people who live in and visit Calgary. You do not have to be an outdoorsy health nut to enjoy urban hiking. Whatever your interest, you will find a hike in this book that suits you. All you need is a sense of adventure and a willingness to explore.

Cultural diversity adds character to Calgary's neighbourhood treks and sometimes the sights lead you to tempting taste experiences. For example, take a hike through Little Italy in the northeast community of Bridgeland, which is set on a hillside overlooking the Bow River. Trekking through Bridgeland takes you along tree-lined streets, past wartime homes and abundant summer vegetable gardens. Work up a sweat (and an appetite) on the stairs and hills that take you to views of Calgary's downtown core, the Bow River, and the Rocky Mountains to the west. Stop en route for some bruschetta and a baguette at the Italian store, pick up lunch at the fresh pasta shop, or indulge in a full meal at one of the many Italian restaurants.

Maybe you would like to get away from the city's hustle and bustle. Step away from your car, leave your cell phone behind, and trek the grassy paths on the high plateau of Nose Hill. Nature enthusiasts rave about the plant diversity in Nose Hill Park. A sensory explosion of vibrant wildflowers and earth-toned grasses surround hikers from spring to fall.

Geologists point out the glacial erratics, large boulders that have been transported hundreds of miles by glaciers. Archeologists bring your attention to the shiny spots on these boulders, worn and polished where the buffalo rubbed and scratched. The presence of aboriginal artifacts and teepee rings provides another reason to take to the trails on the hill. Or, if you just need to burn off some energy, grab your hiking poles and descend into the deep, tree-filled coulees. The climb back out is sure to leave you breathless! Throughout your hike, the Rocky Mountain vistas, howling coyotes, and city views give you reason to stop, look, and listen while you catch your breath.

Urban hiking is a great way to spice up your city life. Get out of a rut, see something new, and have an adventure close to home. Take to the trails and explore!

TEN GREAT REASONS TO TAKE AN URBAN HIKE

1. **Maintain health and fitness.** Walking outdoors is enjoyable, easy, and one of the best ways to maintain a moderate level of fitness. Choose a lifestyle, not a gym, and you are sure to stick with it in the long run!

2. **Appreciate solitude and nature.** Slow down and take a leisurely stroll on trails far from the hectic pace of the city (e.g., Weaselhead or Fish Creek Park) where you can appreciate the peace, quiet, and beauty of nature.

3. **Train for your next big hiking trip.** The best way to train for hiking is to grab your backpack and hike! The treks in this book are filled with stair- and hill-climbing options for cardiovascular training, and uneven terrain to challenge and improve your balance.

4. **Explore with your kids.** What better way to get fit postpartum than to put baby in a backpack and hit the trails. Take young children on hikes with single-track trails, waterfalls, and chickadees. This is a great way to wear them out and keep you fit!

5. **Get some great gardening ideas.** Full, flowery landscapes are scattered throughout the neighbourhood hikes.

6. **Stop at a coffee shop.** Use urban hikes as an excuse to go to a funky coffee shop with a friend.

7. **Give your dog a change of scenery.** If your dog is sick of sniffing the same old dogs at your local off-leash park or you need some new scenery, then bring your leash and do a combination of on- and off-leash hiking during an urban hike.

8. **You don't have time to go to Banff!** When you really need to get away from the hectic city pace, but don't have a free day to head to the mountains, then hike one of the many "nature" urban hikes.

9. **Burn off some holiday calories.** Take to the trails after you have indulged in a Bernard Callebaut Easter bunny or the second helping of Thanksgiving turkey dinner. A Christmas-lights hike followed by a hot drink at a cozy coffee shop is a perfect pick-me-up and a fun family outing on the long dark nights of the holiday season.

10. **You never knew you could hike in Calgary!** Have a walking adventure close to home!

2

Trail Training

Urban hiking is the perfect activity for helping you to maintain a basic level of fitness. It is good for you and it is enjoyable—the best of both worlds! In this chapter, information about how to hike safely is presented for people adopting an active lifestyle. As well, training ideas are presented for those who are using urban hiking as preparation for more physically demanding pursuits. The cardiovascular fitness you achieve when hiking in the city allows you to tackle more demanding outings with strength and confidence.

Aerobic and Anaerobic Exercise

Being able to breathe comfortably makes an activity much more enjoyable for most people, so before hitting the trails, it is important to understand the role oxygen plays in providing energy. The terms aerobic and anaerobic refer to whether or not oxygen is involved in creating energy for your body while exercising. Moderately intense activities that are repetitive and of prolonged duration, such as hiking, swimming, snowshoeing, and jogging, are aerobic and consume oxygen in the process. Intense activities of short duration, such as sprinting or a steep, quick hill climb on a bike, are usually anaerobic and occur without the benefit of oxygen. These activities will take your breath away.

Aerobic and anaerobic conditioning are complementary. Aerobic conditioning prepares the body for activities of a longer duration, whereas anaerobic training increases the body's ability to climb stairs and hills at a faster pace. If you are new to fitness, then stick with aerobic activity until you've progressed to the point where a muscle burn or lack of oxygen while climbing a flight of stairs sounds like fun.

HEART-SMART HIKING

When you start an exercise program after a period of inactivity, use the "talk test" to measure how hard you are working. If you can inhale enough air to talk comfortably while you are exercising, then you are working at 50 to 70% of your maximum heart rate. SLOW DOWN if you cannot talk. You should never feel dizzy or nauseous while performing any physical activity.

Three Steps to a Successful and Enjoyable Outdoor Fitness Experience

Step 1: Determine Your Maximum Heart Rate

A person's heart rate, measured in beats per minute, is used to evaluate the intensity of an activity. To determine an optimum training intensity for your exercise program, you must first calculate your maximum heart rate, which is the maximum number of times your heart contracts in one minute. For people over 40 years old who are starting an exercise program of moderate to high intensity and for those who have a history of heart problems, the safest way to determine your maximum heart rate is by having a doctor-monitored stress test. For others, a commonly used formula for calculating maximum heart rate is: 220 minus your age. For example, if you are 40 years old, your maximum heart rate is 180 beats per minute.

Step 2: Choose an Appropriate Level of Activity (Training Heart Rate)

Once you have calculated your maximum heart rate (see Step 1), you can estimate an optimum training heart rate using the following calculations:

for low fitness level:
maximum heart rate multiplied by 0.60 (60%)
(e.g., [220-40] x 0.6 = 108 beats per minute, for a 40-year-old)

for average fitness level:
maximum heart rate multiplied by 0.75 (75%)
(e.g., [220–40] x 0.75 = 135 beats per minute, for a 40-year-old)

for athlete:
maximum heart rate multiplied by 0.90 (90%)
(e.g., [220-40] x 0.9 = 162 beats per minute, for a 40-year-old)

As you can see, it is safe to start an exercise program at 60% of your maximum heart rate, but if you want more specific training guidelines with defined benefits, use the zone ratings described in the following table.

> **GET FIT FOR DAY-HIKING IN THE ROCKIES**
> So, you are heading to the hills for some full-day or overnight hiking. Get physically prepared on city hikes by increasing the elevation gain (optional stairs and hills) and carrying a backpack. Fill your backpack with most of the items you will need on a day hike and load the pack properly, placing heavy objects against your back to keep the centre of gravity above your pelvis. Never carry more than one-third of your body weight.

ZONE	ZONE NAME	% OF MAXIMUM HEART RATE	BENEFIT
1	Low intensity and weight control	50–60%	A good zone for beginners to build their cardiovascular foundation and burn fat. Walking, swimming, and biking on flats are activities that keep your heart rate in this zone.
2	Weight control and aerobic maintenance	60–70%	Burns lots of fat and maintains basic fitness level. Endurance activities such as hiking, swimming, jogging, and biking fit into this zone.
3	Aerobic conditioning	70–80%	Improves cardiovascular strength. You feel out of breath, but your muscles do not burn in this zone. Add some hills to hiking, biking, and jogging, or swim some fast laps to reach this zone.
4	Anaerobic	80–90%	Training in the aerobic zone improves your muscular endurance for future physical pursuits. Interval training (adding short bursts of speed to an activity) is an effective way to reach an anaerobic training level. A fast hill climb or a sprint that makes your muscles burn and leaves you gasping for air are in this zone.
5	Insanity	90–100%	The zone name says it all!

Step 3: Monitor Your Fitness Progress (Resting Heart Rate)

As your level of fitness improves, your resting heart rate decreases. Knowing your resting heart rate is a good way to monitor your fitness progress. Take your resting heart rate before you get out of bed in the morning or when you are relaxed. To measure your heart rate, hold the palm of your left hand facing upwards and place two or three fingers from your right hand on your left wrist. Find your pulse and count the beats for 15 seconds. Multiply this number by four to get your heart rate in beats per minute. You can also use this technique to measure your heart rate while you are exercising.

FAT AS FUEL

If you want to burn fat, then perform aerobic exercise at low to moderate intensity (at 50 to 70% of maximum heart rate) for at least 45 minutes at a time. Hiking in Calgary is the perfect aerobic fat burner!

SHIN SPLINTS

Avoid shin splints, a painful inflammation of the shin muscles, by tapping your toes on the ground before heading out on the trails.

HIKING DOWNHILL

Hiking downhill demands that your lower body slow you down while gravity pulls your upper body forward. Decrease the chance of kneecap and thigh muscle pain by hiking downhill slowly, by taking lots of breaks, and by using hiking poles on long downhill stretches.

Training Tips for Neophyte Hikers and Hard-Core Backpackers

Before Heading Out

Hikers sometimes experience muscle imbalances that lead to injuries. One common problem is inadequate strength in the upper and lower legs for hiking downhill, which can result in knee problems. The hamstrings in the back of the leg, and the hip and buttock muscles may also be weak or tight. To avoid injuries while hiking, try the following exercises after a 10-minute walking warm-up. They are designed to stretch a variety of important muscle groups and to move joints through a full range of motion. Focus on maintaining a neutral body alignment while stretching.

NEUTRAL SPINE

Ideal body alignment brings the ear over the shoulder, the shoulder over the centre of the hip joint, and the hip joint over the knee and ankle joint. This posture is called neutral alignment. Neutral spine is a term used to describe your back and, therefore, your spine, when it is in its natural, un-arched position. It is important to maintain a neutral spine throughout the day, whether you are sitting, walking, lifting, or exercising.

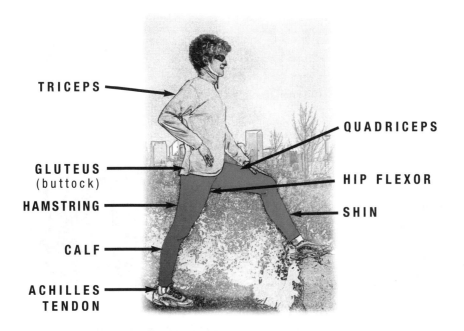

TRICEPS

QUADRICEPS

GLUTEUS (buttock)

HIP FLEXOR

HAMSTRING

SHIN

CALF

ACHILLES TENDON

Calf and Achilles Tendon Stretch

The technique: Place both hands on a vertical surface, such as the trunk of a tree, the back of a bench, or the side of a picnic table. With hands shoulder width apart, keep one leg forward with the knee bent and the other leg extended straight to the back. Both feet should be pointing forward. Feel the stretch in the back of the leg below the knee. Now bend the straight, extended leg until you feel the stretch in the Achilles tendon, which connects the heel with the calf muscles.

The benefit: Maintains flexibility in the calf muscles; helps to prevent Achilles tendon tightness and plantar fasciitis, a sharp pain felt on the bottom of the heel when weight is placed on the foot. Plantar fasciitis is an inflammation of the plantar fascia, a band of tissue much like a tendon, found on the bottom of the foot. The inflammation can become chronic if not treated.

Quadriceps Stretch

The technique: Stand on one foot with your knee slightly bent. Lift the heel of the other foot towards your back. Use your hand, a towel, a bench, or a picnic table to hold your elevated leg in place. Make sure you maintain a neutral spine (do not arch your back) and keep the knees very close to each other.

The benefit: Stretches the quadriceps, which are the large muscles at the front of the thigh, and helps prevent knee and back problems.

Hip Flexor Stretch

The technique: Kneel on the ground on one knee. Bend your other leg in front of you, with the foot flat on the ground. The kneeling leg should be slightly extended, with your knee positioned just behind your buttocks. When you shift weight onto your front leg, the stretch should deepen in your hip flexors, or the top of your thigh. Be careful not to let your front knee go too far forward over your front toes. This puts strain on your front knee. Avoid knee strain by moving your front foot forward. Keep a neutral spine throughout; do not arch your back.

The benefit: Stretches the hip flexors (the muscles that bring your knee toward your chest), which extend from the front of the hip to the lower back and are used to bring the leg forward when walking. Since the hips flexors are tight for most of us, because we sit for much of the day, it is important to keep them well stretched to prevent lower-back soreness.

Hamstring Stretch

The technique: While standing, lift one leg in front of you onto a bench or picnic table seat. With your heel on the bench, point your toes toward the sky. Maintain a neutral spine as you bend forward at the hips with arms extended forward. Feel a pull in the back of the leg, between your buttocks and your knee.

The benefit: Tight hamstrings, which are the muscles at the back of the thigh, can lead to lower back problems. Sitting a lot contributes to tight hamstrings and lower back soreness.

Gluteus (Buttock) Stretch

The technique: In a standing position, bend your right leg and place your right ankle on a bench, picnic table, or on your left knee. The higher the object the more difficult the stretch. Next, bend your left leg as if you are trying to sit down and lean forward from the hips, maintaining a neutral spine, until you feel a stretch in your buttock. For a deeper stretch, push down on the inside of your right knee and hold as you bend forward.

The benefit: The gluteus muscles in the buttock work hard when you step onto high boulders and steps. This stretch maintains their range of motion.

Active Shoulder Stretch

The technique: Bend your arm 90 degrees, lift your hand to chest level, and point your elbow to the side. Circle your arm over your head and back.

The benefit: Stretches the shoulder muscles, and improves or maintains the range of motion in your shoulder joint.

Iliotibial Band (ITB) Stretch

The technique: Stand with your right side facing a tree, wall, boulder, or car and place your right hand on that object, at shoulder level. With your right leg slightly in front of the left, keep both knees slightly bent and bend sideways to the right until you feel a stretch down your left side. For a deeper stretch, move farther away from the object and reach your hand farther above your head.

The benefit: Stretches the muscle and fascia (sheath around the muscle) on the side of the hip, thigh, and knee, which prevents pain at these spots.

Neck and Back Stretch

The technique: Place both hands shoulder width apart on a picnic table, bench, or hood of a car. Keep your feet shoulder width apart and bend forward from the hips. Remember to keep a neutral spine. Relax your head and neck as you drop your head between your arms. If you are using a bench or fence, grab it with your hands, pull back and try to lengthen your spine.

The benefit: This stretch feels great, especially if you have been sitting a lot. It reverses the sitting posture and provides a stretch for the back muscles and chest.

Chest Stretch

The technique: Clasp your hands behind your back and pull down.

The benefit: Stretches your pectoral muscles at the front of your chest and shoulders. These muscles shorten and become tight from sitting for long hours, which can result in headaches or a sore neck.

On The Trail

Hiking in Calgary keeps you fit without the need for additional exercise. However, if you want to challenge specific muscle groups in preparation for an upcoming physical event, then incorporate the following exercises into your urban hike. They complement the fitness benefits of urban hiking and entertain the passersby.

Calf Raises (Flat Surface or Stair Exercise)

The technique. Stand on a flat surface or the edge of a stair. Elevate your body onto your toes. Do three sets of ten elevations and with each set change the position of your feet. Toes in for the first set, toes forward for the second, and toes out for the last. Too easy? Wear your backpack to increase the level of difficulty.

The benefit: Strengthens the lower leg and increases stability in preparation for hiking uphill.

Push-ups (Bench Exercise)

The technique: Place your hands shoulder width apart on a bench, tree, picnic table or car. Two factors allow you to control the level of difficulty of this exercise: the placement of your feet and the height of the bench, tree, etc. Increase the challenge by choosing a bench that is lower to the ground or by doing the push-ups on the ground. Move your feet farther away from your hands to make it tougher, but remember to always keep a flat back (neutral spine) and tight abdominal (core) muscles throughout the exercise. Bring your chest all the way to the object before pushing up. Do two or three sets of ten. At the end of ten you should be fatigued. If you are not, then you need to increase the level of difficulty.

The benefit: Hiking does not use many upper-body muscles. This exercise lets you work your chest and shoulders as well as your abdominal and back (core) muscles.

Dips (Bench Exercise)

The technique: Sit on a bench with the heels of your hands placed on the bench beside you. Move your body off the bench and dip down until your upper arm is parallel with the ground. Make this exercise more difficult by moving your feet farther away from the bench. Always keep your back flat against the bench when

dipping down and back up. Do not dip so far down that you cause discomfort in your shoulders.

The benefit: Increases strength and tones the muscles in the shoulders and upper arm.

Single, Double, and Triple Steps (Stair Exercise)

The technique: Keep your hands free from the rail and step one, two, or three steps at a time.

The benefit: Strengthens the buttock and front of thigh muscles. By keeping your hands free from the rail, your balance is challenged and improved. This is essential for hiking on uneven terrain.

Quadriceps Toner (Hill Exercise)

The technique: Alternate walking forwards and backwards up a gradual slope. Take twenty steps forwards, followed by twenty steps backwards. The bigger the step, the tougher the workout.

The benefit: Strengthens the front of the thigh in preparation for anaerobic demands, such as hiking uphill with a backpack or biking uphill.

After the Hike

Find a tree, bench, or your car and complete the series of stretches from the warm-up. Stretching is a great way to prevent muscle stiffness, allow your heart rate to return to normal, and to give you time to relax and take some deep breaths. Make sure to re-hydrate after the hike with a big glass of water.

3

Clothing, Gear, and Food for Outdoor Activity

The best part about hiking is its simplicity. Urban hiking does not require a lot of special equipment or clothing. However, if you want to take to the trails year round and in all types of weather, then there are a few gear and clothing items that make outdoor activity more comfortable. But before you get dressed for your trek, make sure you fuel up for the long haul.

Fueling Up

Endurance activities such as hiking require a constant supply of energy. Your reserves of fat supply some of the calories needed, but you also need some food in your stomach to keep you from fading too quickly. Enjoy a pre-hike snack that combines carbohydrates and protein. Carbohydrates can be simple or complex. Simple carbohydrates, such as a chocolate bar or piece of white bread, provide lots of sugar, but not much nutritional value compared to the number of calories consumed. Complex carbohydrates, such as multi-grain bread or dried fruit, provide fiber and vitamins along with the sugars you need for energy. As often as possible, choose complex carbohydrates for optimal energy and nutrition. Some proteins have more fat than others, so if you are trying to cut back on fats, then choose low-fat protein options.

SNACK IDEAS FOR HIKING

Pick a combination of protein and carbohydrates.

Protein	Carbohydrates (simple and complex)
nuts (high fat)	dried fruit
cheese (high or low fat)	fresh fruit (e.g., apple, banana, pear)
falafel (a ball of mashed chick peas; high in fat if deep fried)	falafel in pita (the pita supplies simple carbohydrates)
yogurt (low or high fat)	crackers
peanut butter (high fat)	multi-grain bread
meat, fish, hard-boiled eggs	granola bars or cookies

Layers

The best way to keep warm at any time of the year is to layer your clothes. Wearing many thin layers of clothing is much more effective than fewer thick layers, and the type of fabric can make a big difference. Layered clothing keeps you warmer, and allows you to adjust your temperature quickly and easily by adding or removing layers—pretty simple, really!

The Wicking Layer

This is your underwear layer. It is in direct contact with your skin and is responsible for moving moisture away from it. Wicking layers should be made of synthetic materials that are designed to let moisture pass through. They disperse perspiration, so you remain warm even when you are damp. In contrast, cotton underwear traps moisture, which results in chilling.

The Insulating Layer

Your second layer, and possibly third or fourth if it's very cold, traps and reflects heat back towards your body. It should "breathe" so that moisture continues to move through the layers, away from the wicking layer and your body. Fleece, some of which is made from recycled pop bottles, is environmentally friendly and is the best insulating fabric. It consists of millions of fibers and air pockets that trap warm air molecules. Thus, it keeps you warm even when it is wet, and it dries very fast. Wool is also good at insulating, but it doesn't dry as fast as fleece does, and is quite heavy when wet. Again, cotton is evil!

HATS AND NECK WARMERS

Because you lose a lot of heat through your head (some say from 40 to 60%), an easy way to warm up quickly is to put on a hat and neck warmer. When you get too hot, just remove them!

The Shell Layer

This final, outer layer protects your body against wind, rain, and snow. When buying a shell jacket, you must ask yourself what your needs are. Will you be out in the elements, far away from home, where a downpour could make your life miserable? If so, a more expensive, waterproof, breathable jacket will make your life more comfortable. Or will you be hiking in the city, always close to a cozy coffee shop? If this is the case, a less expensive wind/rain resistant or waterproof jacket will do the trick.

There are three types of outerwear available for hikers to choose from, each with advantages and disadvantages.

Wind-proof/water-resistant: These are light jackets that provide protection from the wind. They will keep you dry in a soft drizzle, but are ineffective in a downpour.

Waterproof: These are rubbery rain outfits that do not "breathe." If you perspire under the jacket, your sweat will eventually soak you. However, rain jackets with zippers under the armpit (pit zips) offer some ventilation. Also, since your legs don't sweat as much as your torso does, pants in this fabric work fine, especially if they have zippers down the leg to allow some air circulation.

Waterproof/breathable: These high-end jackets are waterproof and can "breathe," with holes between the fibers that are small enough to keep rain droplets out, but big enough to let vapour from sweat escape. One familiar brand name is Gore-tex® but there are many others, such as Entrant®, Extreme®, Hydroflex®, and Ultrex®. All brand name products are either two-ply or three-ply. Two-ply clothing has an outer layer of fabric with a water-repellent coating and an inner layer of waterproof breathable urethane or polyurethane. The three-ply clothing has a third layer of fabric on the inside. Jacket fabrics can be heavy and stiff for those who tend to rub against rocks (good for buffalo) or the fabric can be light and flexible for less rigorous use. The fabric has a treatment that keeps rain from soaking into the fibres. When this treatment wears off, particularly on your shoulders where your pack sits, rainwater will soak in and the fabric "wets out". You will get wet wherever the jacket wets out, since your sweat will not be able to escape through the wet fabric. The jacket is not broken, it just needs to be retreated with a spray or wash-in treatment that you buy at an outdoor store.

Socks

Cotton socks work fine on short city hikes in the summer, but in cooler weather it is better to wear a synthetic/wool blend. Socks with padding under the heel and ball of the foot are nice in cool weather and for long outings. To avoid blisters, wear two pairs of socks—a very thin polyester-type liner sock and a thicker, outer sock. The thickness depends on the temperature outside. And remember to wear your sock combination when buying boots.

Footwear

If you have money for only one piece of hiking gear, then buy good footwear. A pain in the foot will guarantee a miserable hike. When trying on boots, it is crucial to be fitted properly. Reputable outdoor stores have a hill-climbing area for testing boots. Some problem areas to watch for include whether your ankle rises and falls when climbing, whether your toes touch the front of the boot upon descent, or whether you have so much room in the front of your boot that, when descending the test hill, your foot gains momentum and jams into the front of the boot. This is known as "toe jam." Ouch!

WHAT DO YOU WANT IN A BOOT?

Good price. Unless a quality brand name is on sale, you get what you pay for. Don't skimp on footwear. These boots have to support your entire body weight while pounding on pavement, hiking gravel-covered pathways, or climbing soggy slopes. Avoid injury and get good footwear!

Ankle support and stability. A stiff boot is a supportive boot. The support comes from the shank that runs along the bottom of the boot. Very stiff boots have full shanks, less stiff boots may have half a shank, and running shoes are shankless. The height of the boot around the ankle also adds support, but not as much as the shank does. Grab a boot at the toe and heel and try to twist it from side to side. The more it twists, the less support it offers.

Light and airy feeling. Challenge the muscles in your feet by wearing light shoes or boots. Whereas stiff boots are heavy and do a lot of the work for your feet, light footwear doesn't weigh you down, but it also doesn't offer any help for balance and stability.

Waterproofness. Full-leather boots are waterproof and the fewer pieces of leather used to make a boot, the better for waterproofness. Gore-tex® boots are also waterproof, but they are extremely hot with almost no breathability. Leather varies in its look, texture, and quality. "Smooth out" leather is smooth, "rough out" is the reverse side of smooth leather, and "suede" looks like "rough out," but isn't. Suede is very easy to break in, but is not as durable as the other two. Rough-out and smooth-out boots need to be treated with a beeswax leather protector whenever they get wet, and on a regular basis to keep them crack-free and waterproof.

Traction on ice: No boot can stop you from slipping on ice. However, the more the tread looks like a snow tire's, the more traction you will get on hard-packed snow, wet pavement, and gravel-covered slopes.

Backpacks

Since an empty backpack always feels comfortable, it is important to put weight in the pack and walk around the store before you buy.

Backpacks for Urban Hikes

If the sole purpose of this pack is for 1- to 3-hour hikes in the city, then a small 10- to 30-litre daypack is perfect. Since you won't be carrying much on these hikes, the fit of the pack is less important.

Backpacks for Longer Hikes

If you are using the same pack to train in the city and hike longer distances, then fit becomes very important.

Hiking Poles

Avoid knee injuries and get an upper-body workout by hiking with two poles. Whether you use old ski poles or specialized hiking poles, you will increase calorie-burn, enjoy improved downhill stability, and significantly reduce the lower-body impact of hiking.

As you press the poles down and away behind you, you will feel your abdominal, back, and arm muscles getting a workout too.

DUCT TAPE AND HIKING

Here are some practical uses for this magical Canadian invention. Note how it is versatile, both grammatically and in its uses. Duct tape can be used as a noun ("*grab the duct tape will ya*"), a verb ("*just duct tape it!*"), and as an adjective ("*I'm all duct taped out*").

Blister preventer. No joke! When breaking in new boots, put a big piece of tape on the back of each heel and around the big and baby toes. Make sure you put the tape on BEFORE a blister appears, and get rid of any hair in the area before applying the tape. Enough said.

Backpack, boot, and jacket repair. Have you got a rip in your pack or Gore-tex® jacket? Just duct tape it. Is the sole of your boot falling off in the middle of your hike? Just duct tape it!

Hiking poles grip enhancer. When using old ski poles that do not adjust in length, wrap some duct tape or hockey tape lower down on the pole for gripping, so you can effectively shorten the pole when climbing.

4

The Hikes

Since May 1997, I have guided Calgarians on urban and mountain hikes in Alberta. Because there was no such thing as urban hiking when I began my guiding career, I set out to create the routes in this book using the following criteria.

Neighbourhood treks with character. Many of the hikes travel through Calgary's older communities, where post-wartime homes are set on tree-lined streets that wind from river valley to ridgetop. Well-to-do neighbourhoods are architecturally interesting and feature gardens galore. Other neighbourhood treks are spiced up with mini-parks, challenging training stairs, and great views of the downtown core and the Rocky Mountains.

Hikes with year-round appeal. Since I believe that a daily dose of fresh-air activity is crucial to leading a sane and happy life, no matter what the time of year, the routes is this book cover all seasons. Spring is the perfect time for training on the trail-training hikes. Sunny and warm, summer speaks for itself! If you want to avoid the summer crowds, then visit Fish Creek for an autumn-colour trek. When the snow starts to fall and the days are short, keep your spirits alive and enjoy a Mount Royal hike through well-lit streets. On a blue-sky day in January, treat yourself to a winter-wonderland walk near the Glenmore Reservoir, followed by a coffee – shop stop.

Getting off the beaten path. As much as possible, the routes in this book get you off the bike paths and onto the earthy hiking trails that are hidden in parks and scattered throughout neighbourhoods. You see fewer people this way and can spend more time enjoying the scenery than avoiding cyclists and rollerbladers.

From neighbourhood garden walks in summer, to stair and hill-training treks, and from evening outings in winter to solitary strolls in Calgary's parks, the route combinations are endless. Be creative when you hit the trails. Happy hiking!

Categories

Each hike has been classified into one or more of the following categories.

CATEGORY	EXPLANATION
Park	Route follows paths in a park or green space.
Neighbourhood	Route follows sidewalks through a neighbourhood.
Park/Neighbourhood	Route is a combination of narrow hiking paths through parks and sidewalk strolls.
Nature	Route offers more solitude than the park routes. Wildlife, birds, and wildflowers are a big part of these hikes.
Trail Training	Stairs and hills along these hikes allow for physical conditioning.
Coffee Shop	A cozy café is suggested for a post-hike pick-me-up.
Kids	Kids like these hikes. Routes may follow narrow paths through trees, take you close to a creek, or be full of chirpy chickadees that land on your hands.
Historic	Hikes lead through some of Calgary's older neighbourhoods where historic buildings still stand.
Christmas Lights	Hike routes are great for viewing Christmas lights in December.

Degree of Difficulty

Pacing is the key to an enjoyable hike. You can slow down, have a conversation, and make hills and stairs easy and enjoyable, or you can speed up, carry a backpack, breathe heavily, and feel a burn in your legs. Be sure to review Chapter 2 prior to choosing a hike if you have been inactive for awhile. You should never feel nauseous or light headed when exercising. Listen to what your body tells you and have a safe and enjoyable hiking experience.

FITNESS LEVEL OF HIKE	EXPLANATION	CHOOSING A HIKE FOR YOUR FITNESS LEVEL *(see page 5 for zone details)*
Easy	Mostly flat; almost all hilly parts are optional.	If you are just starting an exercise program, choose a hike at this level and keep your heart rate in Zone 1. You should always be able to carry on a conversation while exercising in this zone.
Moderate	A combination of flats and mandatory hills; may also have optional hills.	When the easy hikes become quite comfortable, try some hikes at the moderate level. It will be quite easy to maintain your heart rate in Zone 1 or Zone 2 throughout the hike. For training on hills, you can exercise in Zone 3 or Zone 4.
Challenging	Lots of hills or stairs that are not optional.	If you participate in regular physical activity (from three to four times a week, for an hour each time) then try a challenging hike. Pick a pace that suits you and have fun!

Trail Etiquette and Safety

Prevent Trail Erosion

I have tried to use established trails in all my routes. Having pointed this out, the City of Calgary Parks Department develops new management plans for parks each year. New trails are developed and old ones are reclaimed to prevent erosion. To keep our parks alive and well for the future, please avoid paths that are closed, even if they are a part of the routes in this book.

Flowers and Wildlife

Stop and smell the flowers, but don't pick them! Leave them for others to enjoy. Never, ever feed the wildlife. Deer, moose, and bear are wild animals and can be dangerous. If you feed them, they may start to demand food from other people, which increases the potential for unhappy encounters between people and wildlife. When animals demand food, they are considered aggressive, dangerous, and a threat to people, and are usually terminated. So don't feed the animals and let them live a long and happy life!

Bike Path Safety

Just as if you were driving, stay on the right-hand side of the path.

Hiking Alone

Seeking peace and solitude is one reason for hitting the urban trails. However, be aware that when you are far from the hustle and bustle, you are also far from help if you need it. Bring a friend or, at the very least, let someone know your planned route before heading out alone.

Hiking in the Dark

When hiking in the dark, bring a friend and a flashlight, wear reflective clothing (Velcro reflective bands for arms and legs are sold at Mountain Equipment Co-op), and follow neighbourhood routes through well-lit streets. For optimal vision at night, try hiking when the sky is clear and the moon is full.

Hiking in Winter and Spring

Be aware that winter brings ice and snow, and spring thaws bring mud. This can lead to slippery sidewalks and paths in these seasons. Take responsibility for your health and safety and wear good footwear, bring hiking poles, and choose an alternate route if you are uncomfortable.

Twelve Mile Coulee, NW

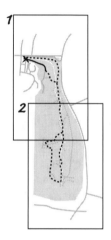

Categories: *trail training, nature, kids*
Approximate Distance: *6 kilometres*
Approximate Time: *1.5 hours*
Degree of Difficulty: *moderate, with one challenging hill climb; lots of optional hill climbs*
Parking: *street parking on Tuscany Hills Crescent or Tuscany Hills Mews; hike starts at the end of Tuscany Hills Mews*
Facilities: *none*

Hike at a Glance

This wild walkabout dips into a coulee that runs parallel to Stoney Trail. Since this area is still part of the Stoney Trail right-of-way and not owned by the city, it has no official status as a park. This means there are no garbage cans for doggie do-do, and the trails are not maintained.

The treed, valley-bottom trail criss-crosses a creek and hides you from the city's hustle. The creek may be dry in the summer and fall, so just imagine the sound of trickling water as you walk along. A long, gradual hill leads you to views of the Rocky Mountains, Canada Olympic Park, and Calgary's city core. Next, the trail loops back to the coulee bottom where you back-track, retracing your steps until the trail turnoff near the end of the trek.

The map is not drawn to scale, but all creek crossings and other narrow paths are marked on the map.

Seasonal Highlights/ Cautions

Spring and Winter: The trails can be slippery and muddy.
Fall: In September, the autumn colours are brilliant.

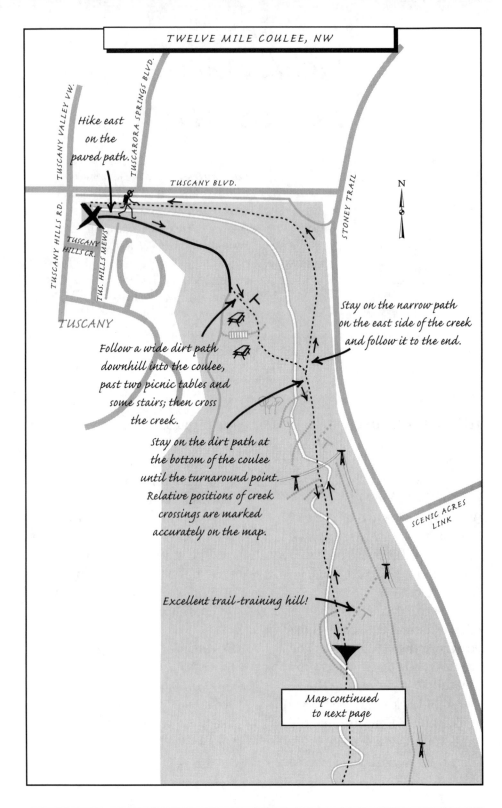

TWELVE MILE COULEE, NW

TUSCANY VALLEY VW.

TUSCARORA SPRINGS BLVD.

TUSCANY HILLS RD.

TUSCANY BLVD.

STONEY TRAIL

N

Hike east on the paved path.

TUSCANY HILLS CR.

TUS. HILLS MEWS

TUSCANY

Follow a wide dirt path downhill into the coulee, past two picnic tables and some stairs; then cross the creek.

Stay on the narrow path on the east side of the creek and follow it to the end.

Stay on the dirt path at the bottom of the coulee until the turnaround point. Relative positions of creek crossings are marked accurately on the map.

SCENIC ACRES LINK

Excellent trail-training hill!

Map continued to next page

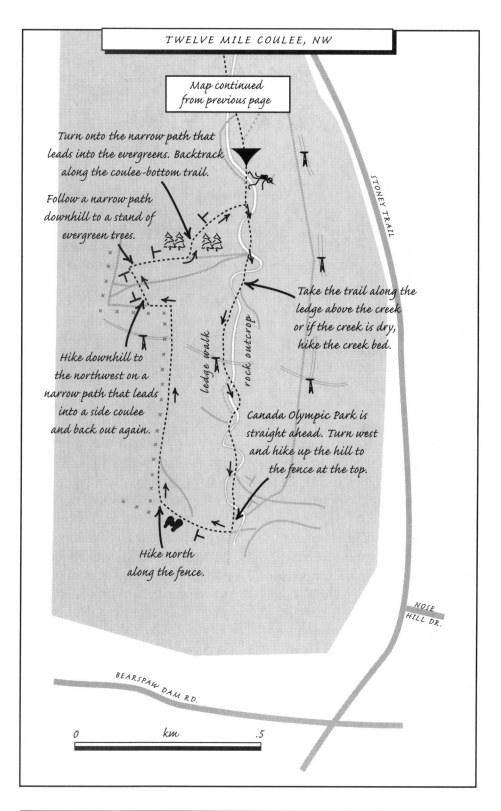

Map continued from previous page

Turn onto the narrow path that leads into the evergreens. Backtrack along the coulee-bottom trail.

Follow a narrow path downhill to a stand of evergreen trees.

STONEY TRAIL

Take the trail along the ledge above the creek or if the creek is dry, hike the creek bed.

ledge walk

rock outcrop

Hike downhill to the northwest on a narrow path that leads into a side coulee and back out again.

Canada Olympic Park is straight ahead. Turn west and hike up the hill to the fence at the top.

Hike north along the fence.

NOSE HILL DR.

BEARSPAW DAM RD.

0   km   .5

Edgemont Park Ravine, NW

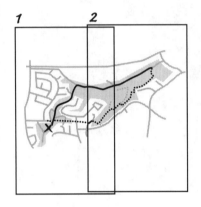

Categories: *trail training, park/neighbourhood*
Approximate Distance: *6 kilometres*
Approximate Time: *1.25 hours*
Degree of Difficulty: *moderate, flat on the way out, with hills on the way back; fantastic hill-training opportunities!*
Parking: *street parking at the end of Edgepark Mews*
Facilities: *none*

Hike at a Glance

Follow paved paths through a mix of manicured and natural coulee parks. In the natural part of the coulee, thick willow shrubs consume the north-facing hillside, preventing haphazard trail creation and maintaining a nice sheltered home for mule deer. Listen for the man-made wetland. Even before you reach the ponds, the bird chatter is loud and clear. Cattails line the water's edge and attract red-winged blackbirds, which have a distinctive call. Next comes the hilly part of the hike, followed by a walk on the grass beside fences bordering the escarpment homes. Not only are the coulee views nice from this vantage point, but by hiking close to these homes, you also give some yippy "guard" dogs a reason to live. The hike continues with another coulee trek on a dirt path and a short jaunt through the neighbourhood. A final hill climb and a set of push-ups on the bench complete the hike.

Seasonal Highlights/ Cautions

All Year: The return loop route follows unofficial dirt and grass paths, some of which are sloped. Good footwear, good balance, and even hiking poles will make hiking these paths more enjoyable.

Summer and Fall: Thistles thrive on parts of the return route from August through October.

The trail is hard to see and is sometimes completely covered in late summer and early fall.

Nature Note

COULEE, RAVINE, OR GULLY?

Calgarians like saying coulee, Maritimers call it a gully, and Yukoners prefer gulch. Here are more names for this landform caused by water erosion: chasm, gap, gorge, ravine, and valley.

The ponds of Edgemont Park Ravine attract a variety of bird life.

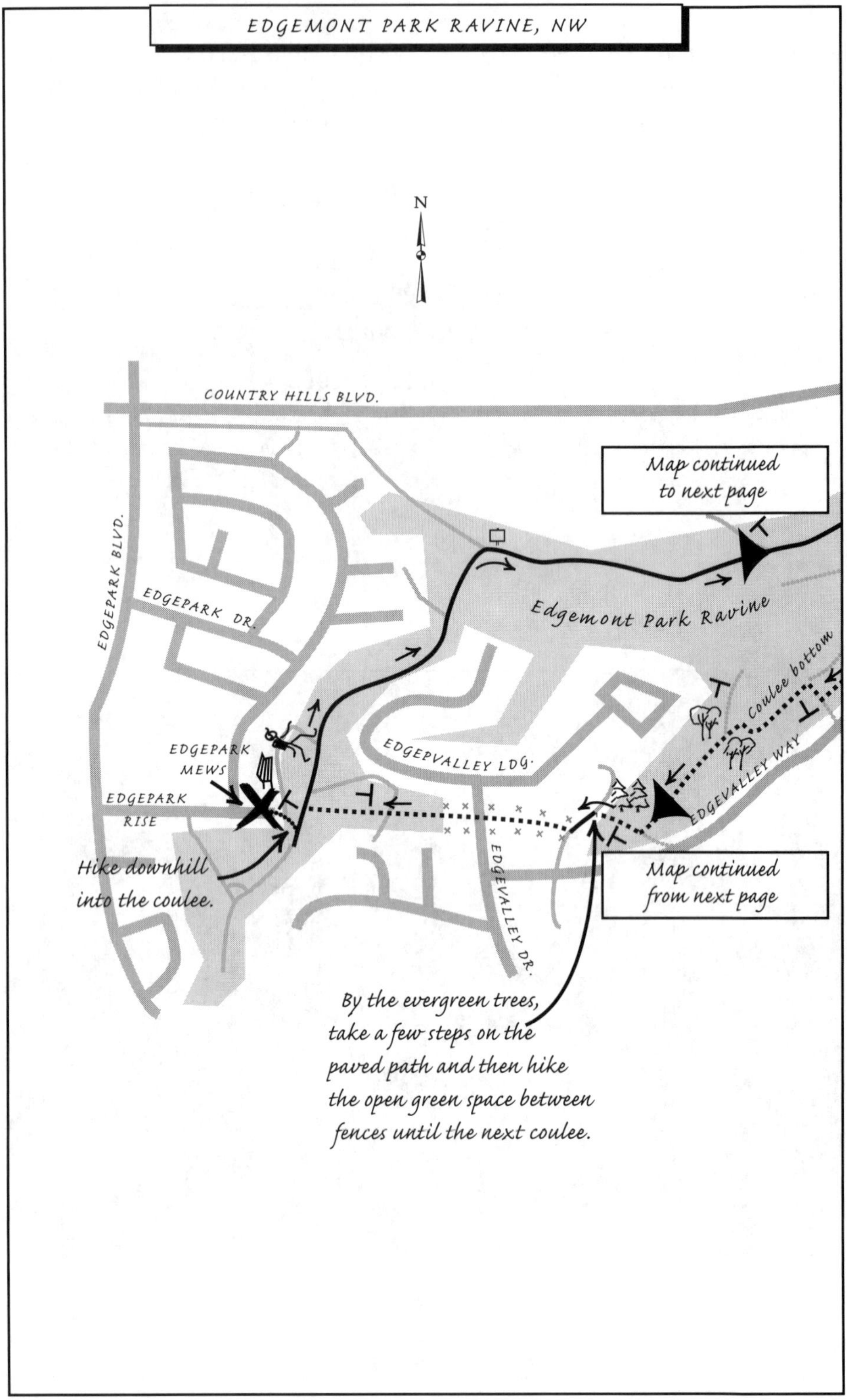
EDGEMONT PARK RAVINE, NW
N
COUNTRY HILLS BLVD.
Map continued to next page
EDGEPARK BLVD.
EDGEPARK DR.
Edgemont Park Ravine
Coulee bottom
EDGEPVALLEY LDG.
EDGEPARK MEWS
EDGEPARK RISE
EDGEVALLEY WAY
Hike downhill into the coulee.
EDGEVALLEY DR.
Map continued from next page
By the evergreen trees, take a few steps on the paved path and then hike the open green space between fences until the next coulee.

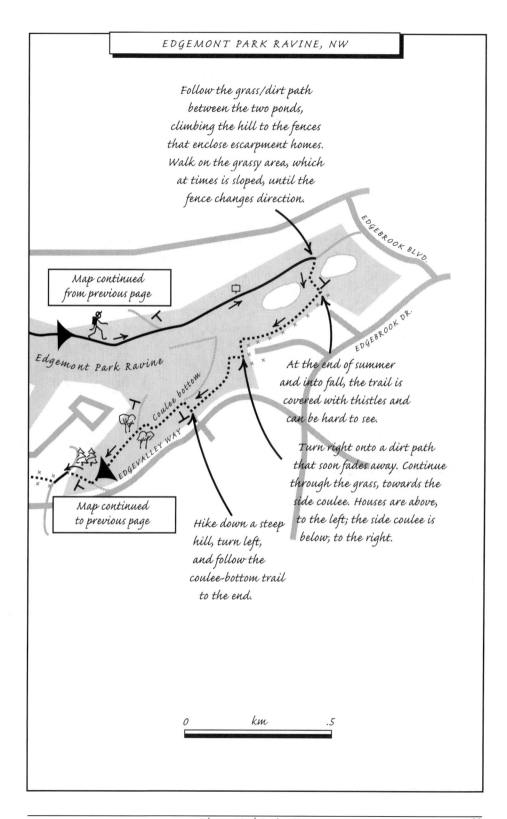

Follow the grass/dirt path
between the two ponds,
climbing the hill to the fences
that enclose escarpment homes.
Walk on the grassy area, which
at times is sloped, until the
fence changes direction.

Map continued
from previous page

Edgemont Park Ravine

Map continued
to previous page

EDGEBROOK BLVD.

EDGEBROOK DR.

Coulee bottom

EDGEVALLEY WAY

At the end of summer
and into fall, the trail is
covered with thistles and
can be hard to see.

Turn right onto a dirt path
that soon fades away. Continue
through the grass, towards the
side coulee. Houses are above,
to the left; the side coulee is
below; to the right.

Hike down a steep
hill, turn left,
and follow the
coulee-bottom trail
to the end.

0   km   .5

Edgemont Hills, NW

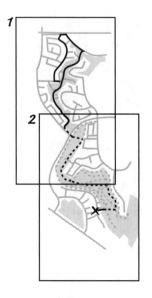

Categories: *trail training, park/neighbourhood*
Approximate Distance: *8 kilometres*
Approximate Time: *1.5–2 hours*
Degree of Difficulty: *moderate, with many optional hills; fantastic hill-training opportunities!*
Parking: *street parking at the intersection of Edgemont Road and the 500 Edgemont Bay*
Facilities: *playground*

Hike at a Glance

Expansive mountain views are just one of the rewards after a long gradual climb up the prairie-grass slopes in the heart of Edgemont. Just west of Nose Hill, this natural area is open to the elements—snowdrifts in winter make it a challenging, yet worthwhile, endeavor. Hike west and explore the collection of dirt paths that criss-cross the hill. Cross Edgemont Boulevard and hike the bottom of a coulee that has been developed into an impressive multi-use park with paved paths and playgrounds. It even has a circuit training area for doing push-ups and pull-ups. Hill-training options are everywhere; however, for those of you who still don't understand my fascination with elevation gains, you can also enjoy a relatively flat trek through a pleasant green space. A short loop along sidewalks in Edgepark gives you a taste of the neighbourhood before you re-enter the coulee and follow your breadcrumbs back to your car.

Seasonal Highlights/ Cautions

Winter: After a big snowfall, snowdrifts can be waist high on the initial hill and street parking can be messy.

Fitness Tip

THE HILL MANTRA

I hope the following items will give you a boost when your mantra changes from "I love hills" to "I hate this guidebook and its warped author."

Cake, beer, nachos! Hiking hills burns a heck of a lot of calories compared to the flat-hike alternative. For example, hiking a 5-degree slope burns twice as many calories as hiking the flats; on a 10-degree slope, you burn three times as many calories and on a 15-degree slope you burn four times the calories.

Peace and quiet! Hills encourage quiet time while you and your hiking pals try to inhale enough oxygen to breathe.

Take your mind off work! Hills let you focus on breathing and the burning sensation in your legs, so all that work stuff just fades away.

Views! Whether it's the view of your friend climbing and panting, the mountains on the horizon, or even a close-up of a tree, you will always be able to find a reason to stop and take a look.

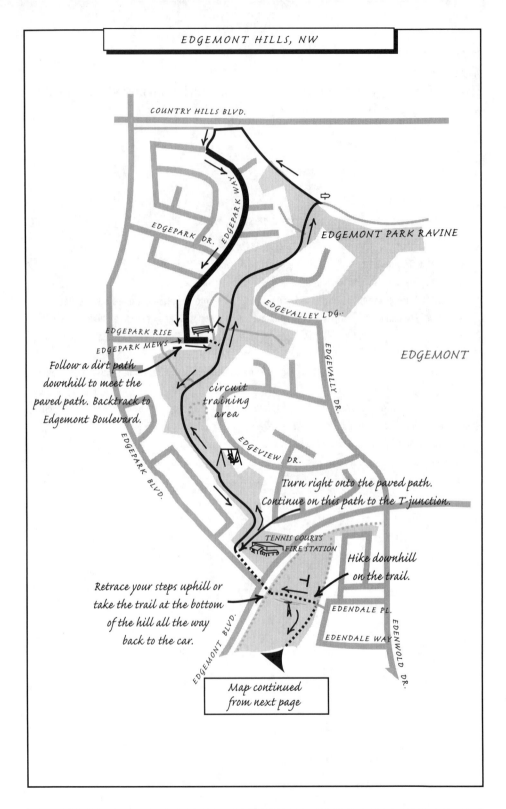

COUNTRY HILLS BLVD.

EDGEPARK DR.

EDGEPARK WAY

EDGEMONT PARK RAVINE

EDGEVALLEY LDG.

EDGEMONT

EDGEPARK RISE

EDGEPARK MEWS

EDGEVALLY DR.

Follow a dirt path
downhill to meet the
paved path. Backtrack to
Edgemont Boulevard.

circuit
training
area

EDGEPARK BLVD.

EDGEVIEW DR.

Turn right onto the paved path.
Continue on this path to the T-junction.

TENNIS COURTS
FIRE STATION

Hike downhill
on the trail.

Retrace your steps uphill or
take the trail at the bottom
of the hill all the way
back to the car.

EDGEMONT BLVD.

EDENDALE PL.

EDENDALE WAY

EDENWOLD DR.

Map continued
from next page

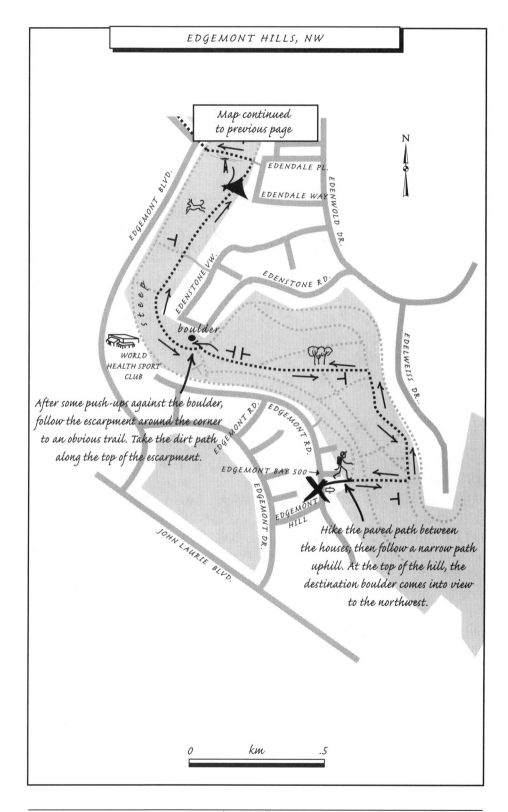

Map continued
to previous page

N

EDENDALE PL.

EDENDALE WAY

EDENWOLD DR.

EDGEMONT BLVD.

EDENSTONE VW.

EDENSTONE RD.

EDELWEISS DR.

steep

boulder

WORLD
HEALTH SPORT
CLUB

After some push-ups against the boulder,
follow the escarpment around the corner
to an obvious trail. Take the dirt path
along the top of the escarpment.

EDGEMONT RD.

EDGEMONT RD.

EDGEMONT BAY 500

EDGEMONT
HILL

EDGEMONT DR.

JOHN LAURIE BLVD.

Hike the paved path between
the houses; then follow a narrow path
uphill. At the top of the hill, the
destination boulder comes into view
to the northwest.

0   km   .5

West Nose Creek Park, NE

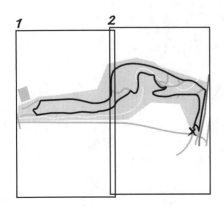

Category: *nature*
Approximate Distance: *6 kilometres*
Approximate Time: *1.25 hours*
Degree of Difficulty: *easy, with gradual hills*
Parking: *official parking lot at the corner of Beddington Trail and Beddington Boulevard*
Facilities: *bathroom (open year round)*

Hike at a Glance

I have nicknamed this hike the "flight path hike." Instead of settling into your vehicle with a Tim Horton's coffee and doughnut to soak up the sights of 747s taking off, why not take a dip into West Nose Creek coulee on a sunny summer's day? Paved paths and a series of bridges lead to a gravel path that follows Nose Creek. Split Rock, a glacial erratic, marks the turnaround point and a climb to the escarpment edge. Several interpretive signs offer historical tidbits about the sandstone quarried from this area. As you hike the return loop along the escarpment edge, watch below for wildlife such as deer and coyotes.

Seasonal Highlights/ Cautions

Winter: The landscape is brown, barren, and not that attractive.

History Note

THE SANDSTONE ERA

It all began in 1886, when a fire consumed much of downtown Calgary. Sandstone subsequently became the building material of choice, and by 1890, over half of the city's tradesmen were stonecutters or masons. During the early 1900s, fifteen quarries operated in the Calgary area and along the Bow and Elbow rivers. Sandstone was used to build schools, large public buildings, churches, and private residences. Many sandstone buildings still stand today and can be seen downtown on 8 Avenue and scattered throughout inner-city neighbourhoods. The rising costs for stone carving combined with poor quality stone and an increase in competition from other building materials led to the closure of many quarries. The outbreak of World War I marked the end of the Sandstone Era.

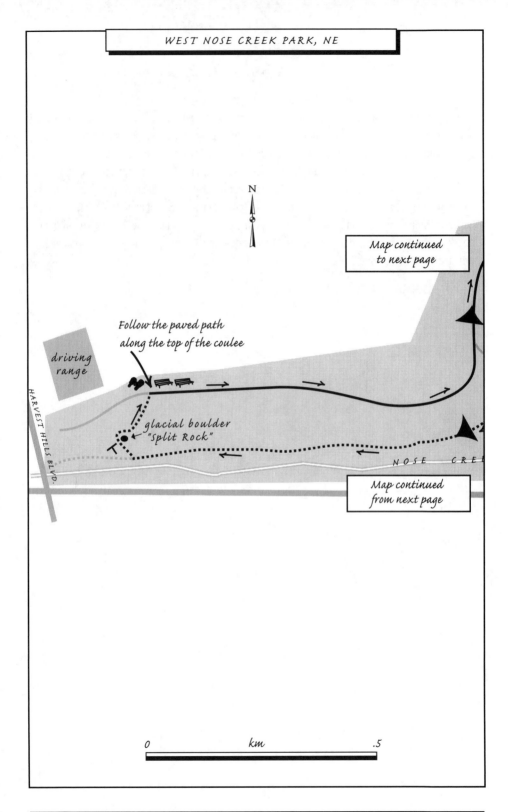

WEST NOSE CREEK PARK, NE

N

Map continued
to next page

Follow the paved path
along the top of the coulee

driving
range

glacial boulder
"split Rock"

HARVEST HILLS BLVD.

NOSE   CREE

Map continued
from next page

0   km   .5

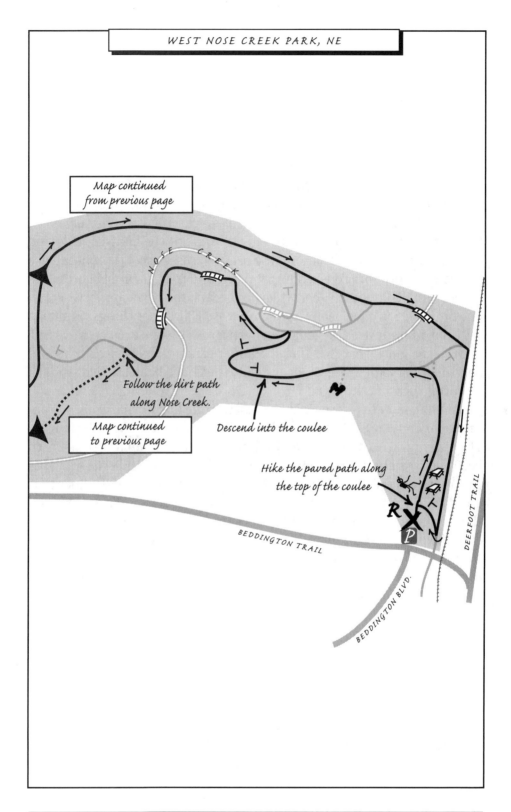

Map continued
from previous page

Map continued
to previous page

Follow the dirt path
along Nose Creek.

Descend into the coulee

Hike the paved path along
the top of the coulee

Nose Hill Park: An Overview

My geologist husband works in the Arctic and when he needs his Arctic fix in Calgary, he heads for Nose Hill Park in the dead of winter. For the remainder of the year, Nose Hill is colourful and alive. The show of colour begins in April with the purple-flowered prairie crocus. Eventually, more than two hundred types of flowering plants dot the landscape during spring, summer, and fall. Among the prairie grasses that dominate Nose Hill, you will also find mushrooms, mosses, and many animals. I often see coyotes and white-tailed deer while hiking. And for all you birders, ninety-one bird species have been sighted on Nose Hill. Other things that keep my hubby happy are the geologically interesting features on Nose Hill, such as the glacial erratics (large boulders transported by glaciers and bearing no resemblance to local rocks) that have been rubbed smooth by buffalo passing through.

At 1,100 hectares, Nose Hill is Canada's largest urban natural environment park and at 1,230 metres, it is the highest point in the Calgary area. The size of the area and the abundant dirt paths mean it is possible to become disoriented. Route Finding 101 suggests using landmarks, such as the mountain ranges in the west, the airport in the east, power lines that cross the hill, the antenna that stands near the quarry on Nose Hill, and the downtown office towers, to ensure that you can find your car at the end of your trek. Using landmarks is also helpful when following the maps provided, since long summer grasses can cover trails, and deer and coyotes can create new ones. By keeping your eyes on landmarks, you can slog through snowdrifts or dip into deep, grass-covered coulees to your heart's content.

This book describes three hikes in Nose Hill Park: Porcupine Valley, Rubbing Stone Hill, and Many Owls Valley. What these hikes have in common is that they all start with a hill climb to the plateau and they all follow dirt paths. All three routes also offer great views! Depending on where you are on the hill, you will see the Rocky Mountain front ranges and foothills, the eastern prairies, the Calgary downtown core, Canada Olympic Park, and the airport. If you are there in the evening and an ambulance drives by with sirens blaring, listen for the chorus of coyotes that is sure to follow. This is urban hiking at its best!

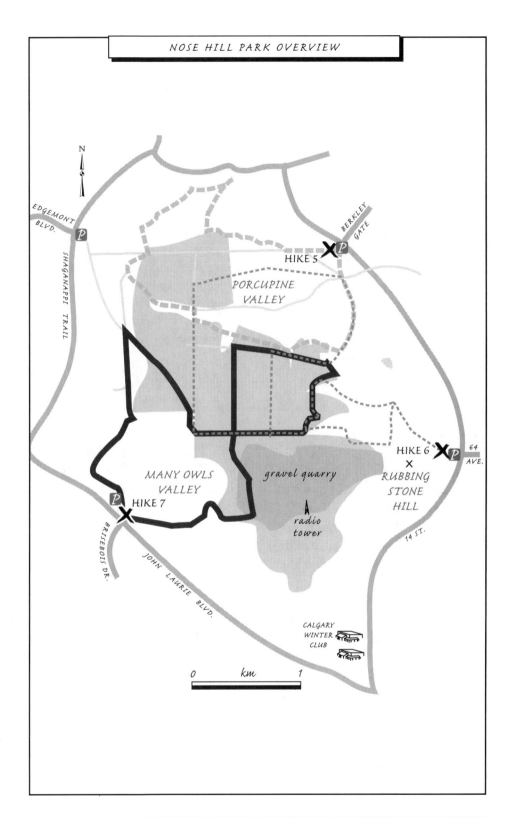

Porcupine Valley (Nose Hill), NW

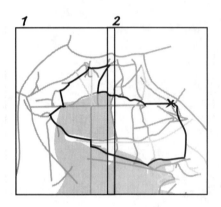

Categories: *trail training, nature*
Approximate Distance: *7 kilometres*
Approximate Time: *1.5 hours*
Degree of Difficulty: *moderate, with some challenging hills; many trail-training options*
Parking: *official parking lot at the intersection of 14 Street and Berkley Gate*
Facilities: *none*

Hike at a Glance

This route is a mix of gradual climbs, flat stretches, and dips into aspen-filled coulees. Aspen groves give shelter to a wide variety of plants and animals from the winds that frequently buffet Nose Hill. While in the coulees, keep a lookout for sheltering great horned owls, American robins, song sparrows, deer, white-tailed hare, and prairie long-tailed weasels. Take to the trails after supper in September when the autumnal hues warm the hill. Burnt-yellow aspen groves, prairie grasses that turn rich red at the tips, and Calgary's trademark big blue sky make this the perfect fall frolic!

Please Note: In the year 2000, the City of Calgary developed a manage-ment plan for Nose Hill. Despite my heroic efforts to follow the city's plan, new trail closures continue to appear on a regular basis. The accessibility of the routes provided may be affected by these ongoing closures.

Seasonal Highlights/ Cautions

Spring: Prairie crocus blooms in April and May. Paths can be muddy in early spring.
Summer: Alberta wildflowers are abundant!
Fall: Rich reds and vibrant yellows cover the hill in September.
Winter: Drifting snow and brisk winter winds make for a challenging hike.

History Note

PREHISTORIC SITES

Forty-two prehistoric archeological sites have been recorded on Nose Hill, including seven teepee rings, a stone cairn/effigy, three stone tool workshops, and fourteen scatters of stone artifacts.

Nature Note

TREMBLING ASPEN CLONES

Parts of Nose Hill are covered with groves of trembling aspens, native trees with round leaves that are easily coerced into movement by the wind. Trembling aspen leaves are fresh green in the spring and turn a vibrant yellow in the fall. Interestingly, all aspens within a grove are genetically identical. The original tree clones itself by sending out suckers from underground roots, each of which becomes a new aspen. Some trembling aspen colonies in Alberta are over 6,000 years old. All clones within a colony change colour at the same time in the fall.

Trembling aspen groves make great hiding spots for animals and add sparkling colour to this grassland hike.

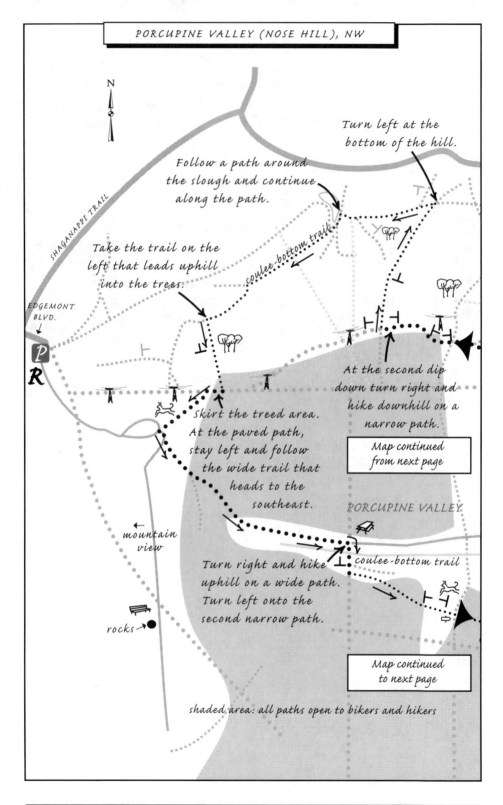

N

SHAGANAPPI TRAIL

Follow a path around
the slough and continue
along the path.

Turn left at the
bottom of the hill.

Take the trail on the
left that leads uphill
into the trees.

coulee-bottom trail

EDGEMONT
BLVD.

P
R

At the second dip
down turn right and
hike downhill on a
narrow path.

Skirt the treed area.
At the paved path,
stay left and follow
the wide trail that
heads to the
southeast.

Map continued
from next page

PORCUPINE VALLEY

coulee-bottom trail

mountain
view

Turn right and hike
uphill on a wide path.
Turn left onto the
second narrow path.

rocks →

Map continued
to next page

shaded area: all paths open to bikers and hikers

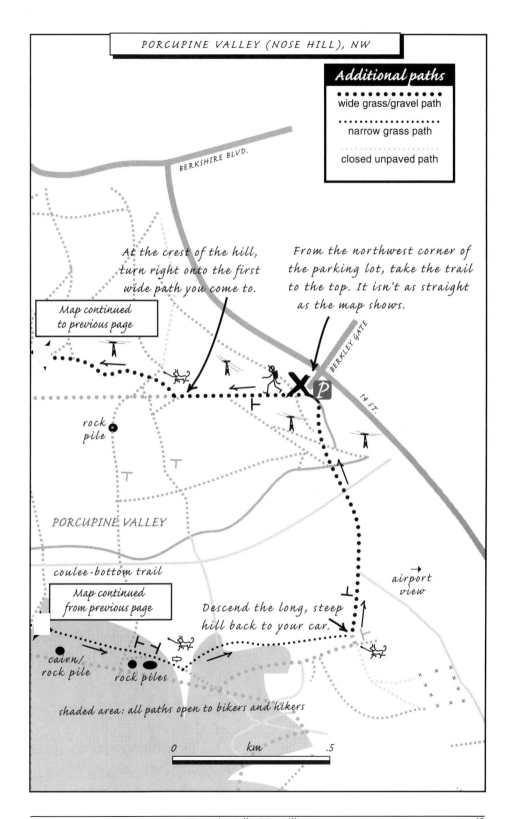

PORCUPINE VALLEY (NOSE HILL), NW

Additional paths

•••••••••••• wide grass/gravel path

·················· narrow grass path

············ closed unpaved path

BERKSHIRE BLVD.

At the crest of the hill, turn right onto the first wide path you come to.

From the northwest corner of the parking lot, take the trail to the top. It isn't as straight as the map shows.

Map continued to previous page

BERKLEY GATE

14 ST.

rock pile

PORCUPINE VALLEY

coulee-bottom trail

Map continued from previous page

airport view

Descend the long, steep hill back to your car.

cairn/ rock pile

rock piles

shaded area: all paths open to bikers and hikers

0   km   .5

Rubbing Stone Hill (Nose Hill), NW

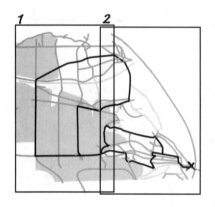

Categories: *trail training, nature*
Approximate Distance: *7 kilometres*
Approximate Time: *1.5–2 hours*
Degree of Difficulty: *moderate, with many challenging hills; many training options*
Parking: *official parking lot at the corner of 64 Avenue and 14 Street*
Facilites: *none*

Hike at a Glance

This is the longest of the Nose Hill routes. It combines dirt paths and old roads, hills and coulee walks. The trail markers on this route date back to the ice age, at least 13,000 years ago. Boulders known as glacial erratics travelled hundreds of kilometres on glaciers before choosing Nose Hill as their resting spot. Humans have also left their mark on the hill by re-arranging the glacially transported stones. There are up to sixty teepee rings on the hill, but you will have to do some independent exploration to see these. So, when you do push-ups or post-hike stretches against that glacial erratic, you are making history.

Future guidebooks will describe the crazy things people did in the twenty-first century while hiking on Nose Hill.

Please Note: In the year 2000, the City of Calgary developed a management plan for Nose Hill. Despite my heroic efforts to follow the city's plan, new trail closures continue to appear on a regular basis. The accessibility of the routes provided may be affected by these ongoing closures.

Seasonal Highlights/ Cautions

Spring: Prairie crocus blooms in April and May. Paths can be muddy in early spring.

Summer: Alberta wildflowers are abundant!

Fall: Rich reds and vibrant yellows cover the hill in September.

Winter: Drifting snow and brisk winter winds make for a challenging hike.

Nature Notes

GRASS FACTS

Hardy grasses dominate the prairies and make up a large part of Nose Hill.

These flowering plants are pollinated by the wind. They have no colourful flowers because they do not need to attract insects for pollination.

Grasses benefit from grazing by large mammals like buffalo and deer. Grazing removes the dead plants (the grass we see aboveground) and allows the sun to reach new growth in the spring.

Seeds eaten by grazing animals are dispersed with their own supply of fertilizer.

ITCHY BUFFALO

When the glaciers carved their way across Nose Hill, they left behind many large boulders known as glacial erratics, which bear no compositional resemblance to local rocks. One hundred years ago, buffalo roamed Nose Hill. In the spring, the buffalo would rub against these stones as they began to molt, trying to remove irritating hairs. You can see the evidence in the form of deep, smooth depressions and shiny spots that remain on the stones today.

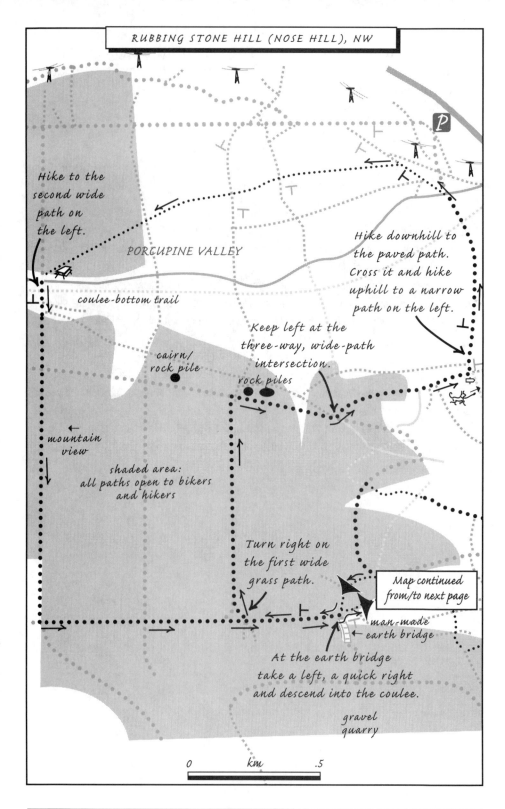

RUBBING STONE HILL (NOSE HILL), NW

Hike to the
second wide
path on
the left.

PORCUPINE VALLEY

coulee-bottom trail

Hike downhill to
the paved path.
Cross it and hike
uphill to a narrow
path on the left.

Keep left at the
three-way, wide-path
intersection.

cairn/
rock pile

rock piles

mountain
view

shaded area:
all paths open to bikers
and hikers

Turn right on
the first wide
grass path.

Map continued
from/to next page

man-made
earth bridge

At the earth bridge
take a left, a quick right
and descend into the coulee.

gravel
quarry

0   km   .5

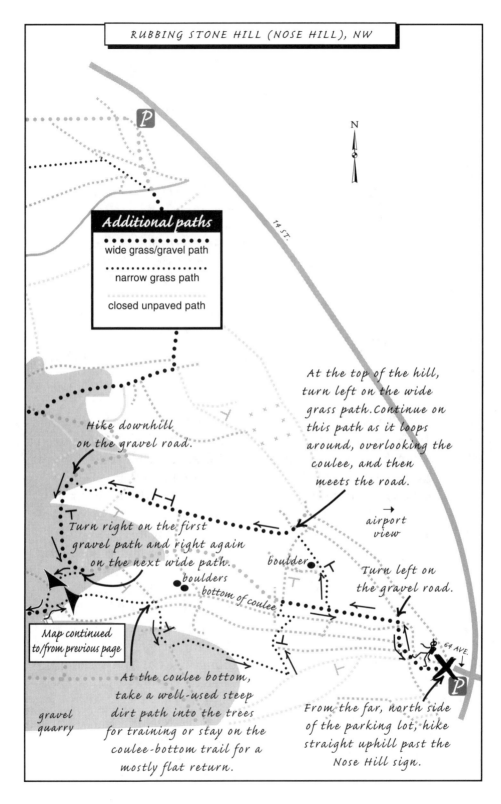

N

Additional paths

●●●●●●●●●●●●●
wide grass/gravel path

••••••••••••••
narrow grass path

∙∙∙∙∙∙∙∙∙∙∙∙∙∙
closed unpaved path

14 ST.

At the top of the hill,
turn left on the wide
grass path. Continue on
this path as it loops
around, overlooking the
coulee, and then
meets the road.

→
airport
view

Hike downhill
on the gravel road.

Turn right on the first
gravel path and right again
on the next wide path.

boulder

Turn left on
the gravel road.

boulders
bottom of coulee

Map continued
to/from previous page

64 AVE.

At the coulee bottom,
take a well-used steep
dirt path into the trees
for training or stay on the
coulee-bottom trail for a
mostly flat return.

From the far, north side
of the parking lot, hike
straight uphill past the
Nose Hill sign.

gravel
quarry

Many Owls Valley (Nose Hill), NW

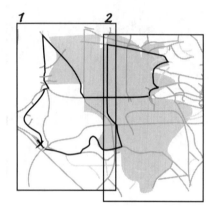

Categories: *nature, trail training*
Approximate Distance: *7 kilometres*
Approximate Time: *1.5 hours*
Degree of Difficulty: *easy and mostly flat, with a couple of long, gradual hills to climb; many hill-training options along the way*
Parking: *official parking lot at the corner of Brisebois Drive and John Laurie Boulevard*
Facilities: *none*

Hike at a Glance

All Nose Hill hikes start with a climb, but for those of you looking forward to some flat trekking, you are in luck. Of course, there is the requisite climb at the beginning of this route, but when you get to the top of Nose Hill, you will notice that the terrain is quite flat. Take a look around and you will see that Broadcast Hill (the hill where Canada Olympic Park is built) is also flat and at the same elevation. Hills south of the city near Priddis are the same. These plateaus are the remnants of a 60-million-year-old swampy, forested landscape into which the Bow and Elbow rivers, and the glaciers that followed their

valleys, have incised by 175 metres. That is something to think about while you catch your breath. Enjoy a flat walk on the plateau from this point forward. Hone your senses while you walk. Listen for coyotes howling at passing sirens and in the spring, summer, and fall, enjoy the colour explosion of wildflowers that you can't see from the road. Purple prairie crocuses and yellow buffalo bean, pink wild roses, orange lilies, and purple lupines dress up the grassy landscape of the hill.

Please Note: In the year 2000, the City of Calgary developed a management plan for Nose Hill. Despite my heroic efforts to follow the city's plan, new trail closures continue to appear on a regular basis. The accessibility of the routes provided may be affected by these ongoing closures.

Seasonal Highlights/ Cautions

Spring: Prairie crocus blooms in April and May. Paths can be muddy in early spring.

Summer: Alberta wildflowers are abundant!

Fall: Rich reds and vibrant yellows cover the hill in September.

Winter: Drifting snow and brisk winter winds make for a challenging hike.

Fitness Tip

BALANCE

With every step you take, you lose, correct, and regain your balance. This is not a problem when the terrain is an ice-free sidewalk, but throw in a few obstacles such as tree roots, gopher holes, or slippery slopes and you will be very aware of your ability to stay upright and injury free. Nose Hill's uneven terrain challenges all the muscles in your feet, thus strengthening your foot muscles, which is the best way to improve your balance.

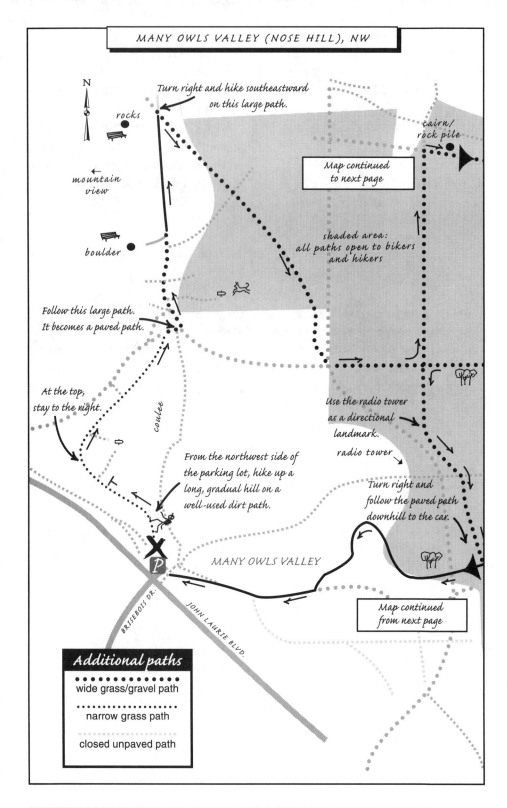

MANY OWLS VALLEY (NOSE HILL), NW

N

rocks

mountain
view

boulder

Turn right and hike southeastward
on this large path.

cairn/
rock pile

Map continued
to next page

shaded area:
all paths open to bikers
and hikers

Follow this large path.
It becomes a paved path.

At the top,
stay to the right.

coulee

Use the radio tower
as a directional
landmark.

radio tower

From the northwest side of
the parking lot, hike up a
long, gradual hill on a
well-used dirt path.

Turn right and
follow the paved path
downhill to the car.

MANY OWLS VALLEY

Map continued
from next page

BRISEBOIS DR.

JOHN LAURIE BLVD.

Additional paths

wide grass/gravel path

narrow grass path

closed unpaved path

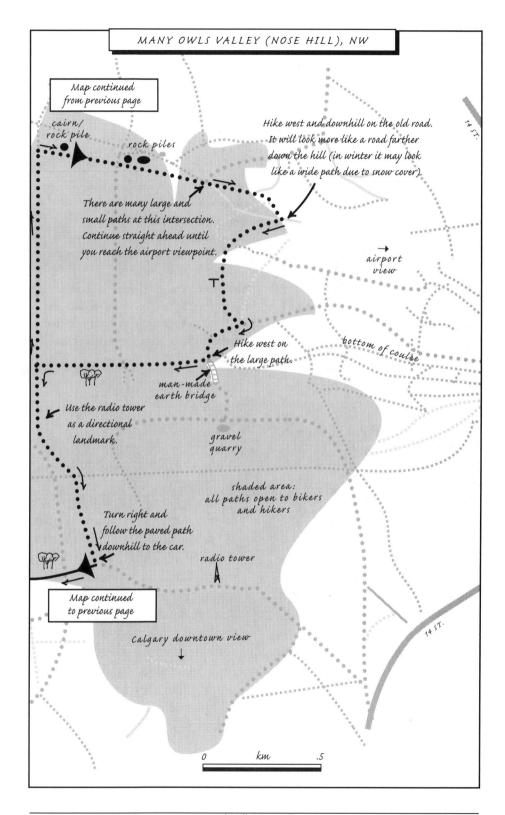

Map continued from previous page

cairn/ rock pile

rock piles

Hike west and downhill on the old road. It will look more like a road farther down the hill (in winter it may look like a wide path due to snow cover).

There are many large and small paths at this intersection. Continue straight ahead until you reach the airport viewpoint.

→ airport view

T

bottom of coulee

Hike west on the large path.

man-made earth bridge

Use the radio tower as a directional landmark.

gravel quarry

shaded area: all paths open to bikers and hikers

Turn right and follow the paved path downhill to the car.

radio tower

Map continued to previous page

Calgary downtown view

14 ST.

14 ST.

0   km   .5

Bowmont Park West, NW

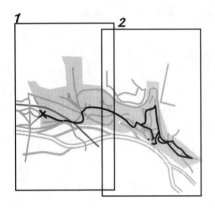

Categories: *trail training, nature, kids*
Approximate Distance: *6 kilometres*
Approximate Time: *1.5 hours*
Degree of Difficulty: *moderate, with lots of rolling hills and some challenging steep hills; many trail-training options*
Parking: *official parking lot on Scenic Bow Road, just off 85 Street; the parking area is a pull-off on a sharp corner; a Bowmont Park sign hangs on the fence at the park entrance*
Facilities: *none*

Hike at a Glance

Grab your hiking poles for this hilly, single-track, dirt-path hike along the Bow River escarpment. You will enjoy views of the Bow River, downtown Calgary, and the Rockies as you dip and climb. If heavy breathing isn't your favourite pastime, then bring a camera, a kid, or a dog and make lots of stops. In the summer, the grasslands are covered with Alberta wildflowers, and in the fall, the shrubs beam with burnt yellows and rich reds. The highlight on this trek is Waterfall Valley. The cascading falls are composed of tufa – mineral deposits that precipitate out of the spring water.

On a very cold, winter day when the falls are frozen and the spring water is warmer than the air, a glacial steam bath welcomes you. You will love this hike!

Please Note: Throughout 2001, the City of Calgary was in the process of developing a management plan for Bowmont Park. A new secondary trail system will encourage users to stay on designated trails, and new on- and off-leash areas for dogs will be developed. The plan will not be complete before this guidebook is published, therefore map accuracy may be affected when the plan is implemented.

Seasonal Highlights/ Cautions

Spring: Trails can be muddy.
Summer and Fall: Alberta wild-flowers are abundant.

Winter: Enjoy the frozen waterfall in Waterfall Valley.

Fitness Tips

POLE IT!

Avoid knee injuries and get an upper-body workout by hiking with two poles on this hilly Bowmont trek. Two poles are better than one because four points of contact make you more stable than three. It is important to adjust pole length to suit the terrain. When hanging onto the pole handle, your forearm should be parallel to the ground. That means you shorten the pole on the climb and lengthen it on the descent. As you press the poles down and away behind you, you will feel your abdominal, back, and arm muscles getting a workout too. Poles not only increase your downhill stability and the number of calories you burn, but they also significantly reduce the impact of hiking on the lower body.

BLOOD AND GUTS

There is a benefit to the burning sensation you feel while hiking uphill. Although a slow and consistent pace is the key to developing endurance, a faster pace will help you build muscle strength and improve your anaerobic threshold (see Hike 18: Edworthy Park). Strong muscles are helpful for supporting your body on steep-slope descents, or for a quick burst of energy.

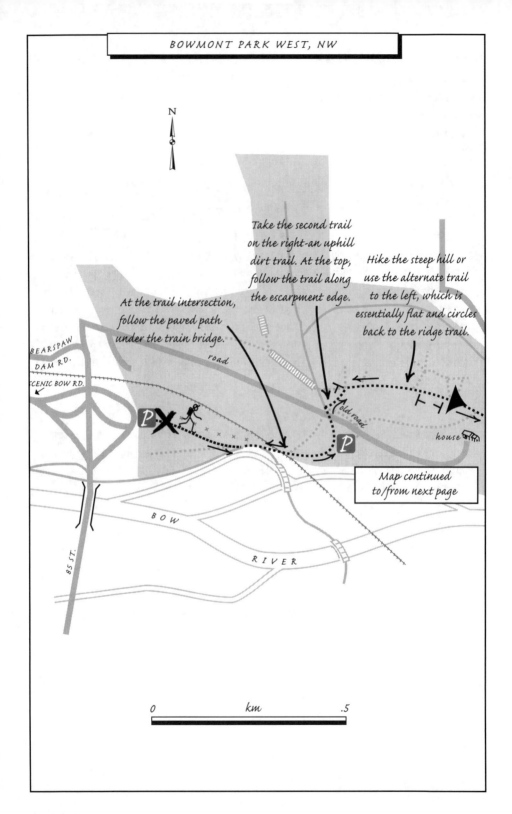

N

Take the second trail on the right-an uphill dirt trail. At the top, follow the trail along the escarpment edge.

Hike the steep hill or use the alternate trail to the left, which is essentially flat and circles back to the ridge trail.

At the trail intersection, follow the paved path under the train bridge.

BEARSPAW DAM RD.

CENIC BOW RD.

road

old road

house

Map continued to/from next page

85 ST.

B O W

R I V E R

0   km   .5

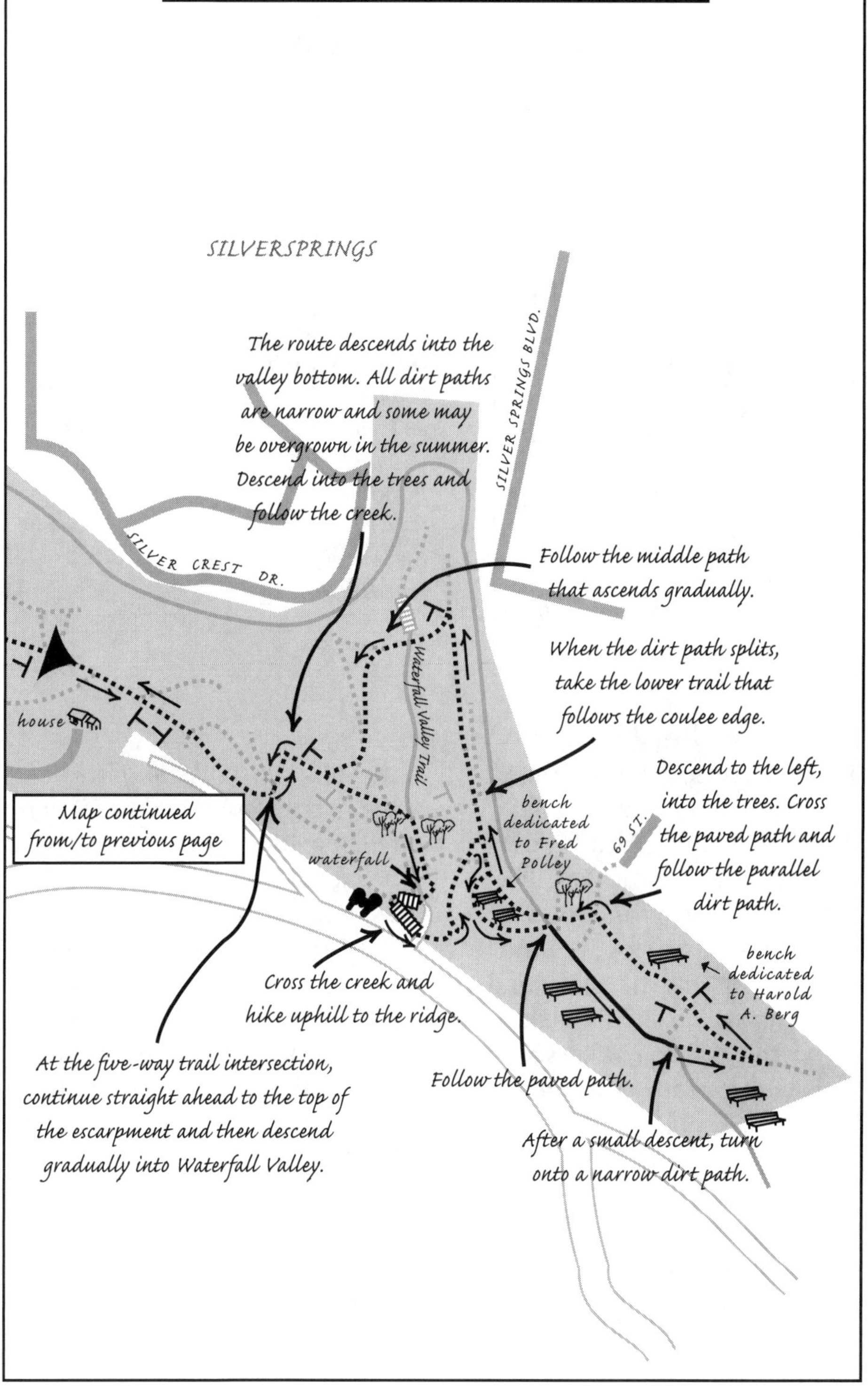

SILVERSPRINGS

The route descends into the valley bottom. All dirt paths are narrow and some may be overgrown in the summer. Descend into the trees and follow the creek.

SILVER SPRINGS BLVD.

SILVER CREST DR.

Follow the middle path that ascends gradually.

When the dirt path splits, take the lower trail that follows the coulee edge.

Waterfall Valley Trail

house

Descend to the left, into the trees. Cross the paved path and follow the parallel dirt path.

bench dedicated to Fred Polley

69 ST.

Map continued from/to previous page

waterfall

bench dedicated to Harold A. Berg

Cross the creek and hike uphill to the ridge.

At the five-way trail intersection, continue straight ahead to the top of the escarpment and then descend gradually into Waterfall Valley.

Follow the paved path.

After a small descent, turn onto a narrow dirt path.

Bowmont Park East, NW

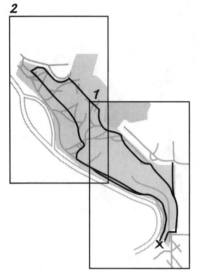

Categories: *trail training, nature*
Approximate Distance: *6 kilometres*
Approximate Time: *1.5 hours*
Degree of Difficulty: *starts easy but becomes moderate, with lots of rolling hills and some challenging steep hills; many training options*
Parking: *official parking lot on 52 Street (one-way), just off Home Road; there is no sign at the parking lot entrance*
Facilities: *none*

Hike at a Glance

Tucked between the community of Silver Springs and the Bow River is Bowmont Park. Hike the paved path along the Bow River before turning off onto dirt paths and grassy slopes. Some runners call this the "blood and guts" run, which should make you happy to be a hiker. Hikers should pace themselves for pleasure on Bowmont's rolling hills, because that is the key to endurance.

This is simply a breathtaking hike, one of my favourites in Calgary. When you need a break from the city, come here to enjoy the hills, the majestic views of the Rocky Mountains, the glacier-fed Bow River (brrrrr!), and the beautiful summer wildflowers.

Please note: Throughout 2001, the City of Calgary was in the process of developing a management plan for Bowmont Park. A new secondary trail system will encourage users to stay on designated trails, and new on- and off-leash areas for dogs will be developed. The plan will not be complete before this guidebook is published, therefore map accuracy may be affected when the plan is implemented.

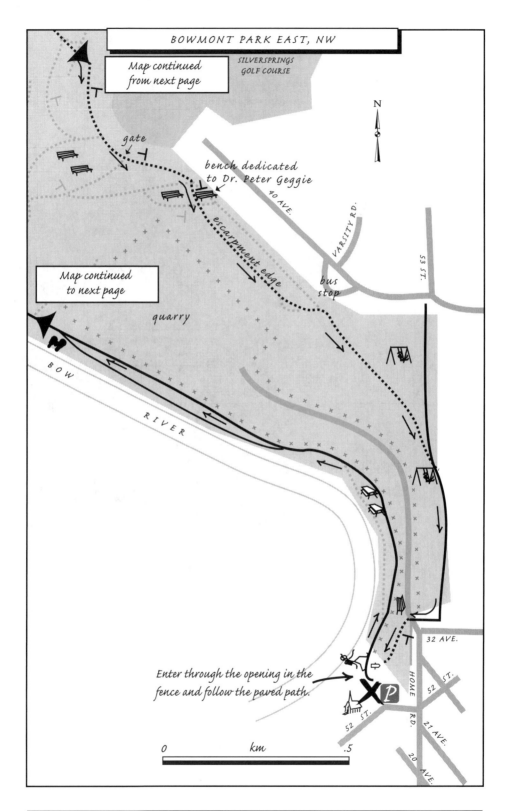

SILVERSPRINGS
GOLF COURSE

N

Map continued
from next page

gate

bench dedicated
to Dr. Peter Geggie

40 AVE.

VARSITY RD.

53 ST.

escarpment edge

Map continued
to next page

bus
stop

quarry

B O W

R I V E R

32 AVE.

HOME

52 ST.

Enter through the opening in the
fence and follow the paved path.

P

RD.

21 AVE.

52 ST.

20 AVE.

0   km   .5

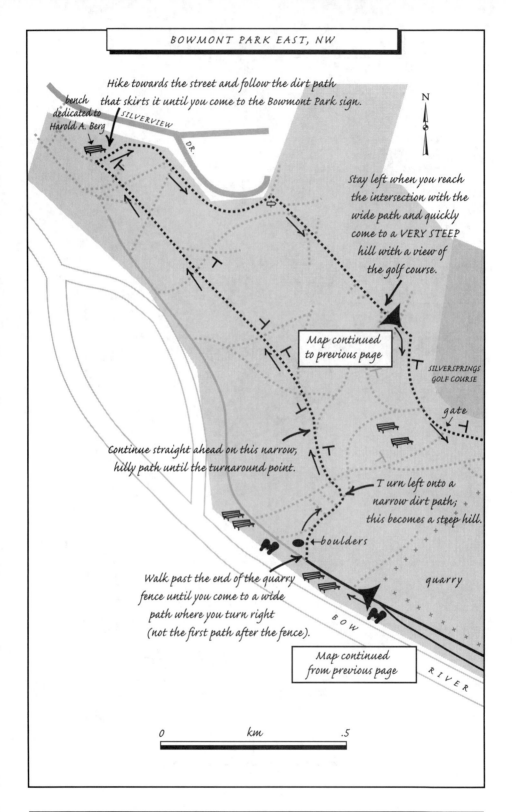

Hike towards the street and follow the dirt path that skirts it until you come to the Bowmont Park sign.

bench dedicated to Harold A. Berg

SILVERVIEW DR.

N

Stay left when you reach the intersection with the wide path and quickly come to a VERY STEEP hill with a view of the golf course.

Map continued to previous page

SILVERSPRINGS GOLF COURSE

gate

Continue straight ahead on this narrow, hilly path until the turnaround point.

Turn left onto a narrow dirt path; this becomes a steep hill.

←boulders

quarry

Walk past the end of the quarry fence until you come to a wide path where you turn right (not the first path after the fence).

BOW RIVER

Map continued from previous page

0   km   .5

Bowness Park/ Bow River, NW

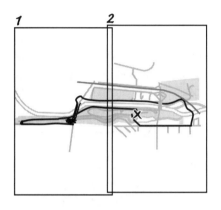

Categories: *trail training, nature, coffee shop, kids*
Approximate Distance: *8 kilometres*
Approximate Time: *1.5–2 hours*
Degree of Difficulty: *easy, with some hills at the beginning, followed by a flat, paved path*
Parking: *from 85 Street, follow the signs to Bowness Park; park in the first parking lot*
Facilities: *bathroom (open from May to September), bathroom near café (open year round); playgrounds; picnic tables; barbecue pits; concession/café (open year round)*

Hike at a Glance

Bowness Park has many trails, but the best one is the hidden, forested path that remains a local secret. The paved path along the Bow River takes you to this treed hike. Climbing dirt paths and stairs elevates your heart rate as you trek through evergreens. Take a breather and enjoy peephole views of the Bow River below before reaching the summit and the neighbourhood of Valley Ridge. Loop back down along the paved path or backtrack through the forest. The short loop passes through a Douglas fir forest on the south side of the lagoon. A longer loop passes under the impressive Stoney Trail and fol-lows the Bow River Pathway, past Baker Park and Bowmont Park, before looping back along sidewalks through Bowness.

Seasonal Highlights/ Cautions

Winter and Spring: The treed trail section at the beginning can be very slippery and icy.

JAVA TEMPTATIONS

Java Temptations is a friendly, family-run café with a full menu of homemade treats. Sweet-tooth snacks include layer cakes, cheesecakes, muffins, and scones, and for lunch, why not try a wrap or quesadilla?
Location: 300, 11245 Valley Ridge Drive NW

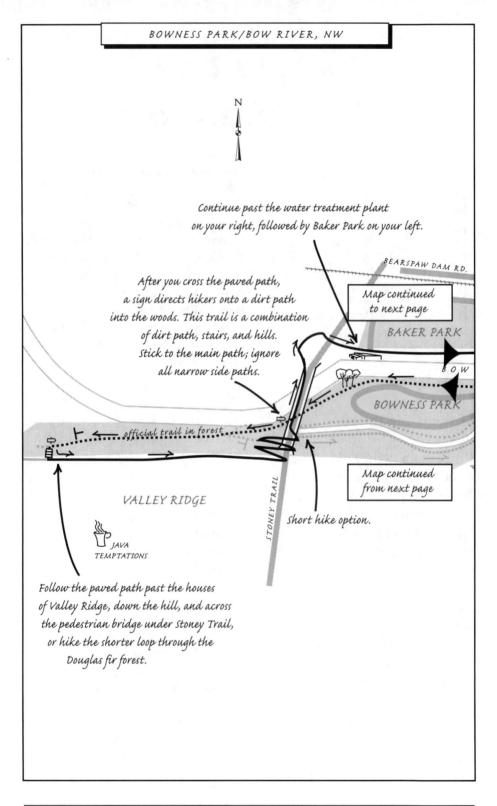

N

Continue past the water treatment plant
on your right, followed by Baker Park on your left.

BEARSPAW DAM RD.

Map continued
to next page

BAKER PARK

After you cross the paved path,
a sign directs hikers onto a dirt path
into the woods. This trail is a combination
of dirt path, stairs, and hills.
Stick to the main path; ignore
all narrow side paths.

BOW

BOWNESS PARK

official trail in forest

Map continued
from next page

VALLEY RIDGE

STONEY TRAIL

Short hike option.

JAVA
TEMPTATIONS

Follow the paved path past the houses
of Valley Ridge, down the hill, and across
the pedestrian bridge under Stoney Trail,
or hike the shorter loop through the
Douglas fir forest.

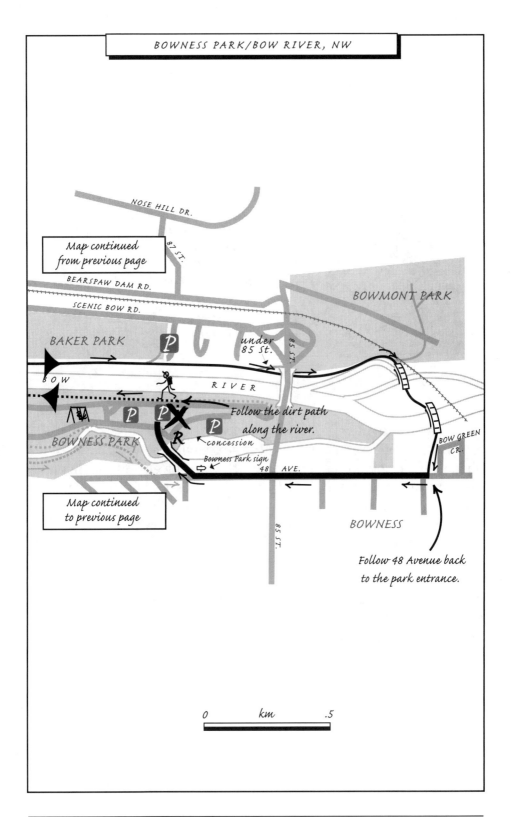

Map continued
from previous page

NOSE HILL DR.

87 ST.

BEARSPAW DAM RD.

SCENIC BOW RD.

BAKER PARK

BOWMONT PARK

85 ST.

under
85 St.

BOW

RIVER

Follow the dirt path
along the river.

BOWNESS PARK

concession

R

Bowness Park sign

48 AVE.

BOW GREEN
CR.

Map continued
to previous page

85 ST.

BOWNESS

Follow 48 Avenue back
to the park entrance.

0   km   .5

Bowness/Shouldice Park, NW

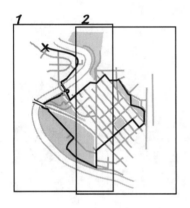

Category: neighbourhood
Approximate Distance: 7 kilometres
Approximate Time: 1.25 hours
Degree of Difficulty: easy, with a few hills
Parking: park on the street at the corner of 61 Street and Bow Crescent
Facilities: bathrooms (open from May to September)

Hike at a Glance

Hike past grand riverfront abodes, exceptionally small wartime homes, and renovated houses of all shapes and sizes. Bowness has homes people live in and despite a few neglected residences and some rusted cars, this is a pleasant sidewalk stroll past owner-landscaped yards and proudly manicured lawns, up to a hilltop green space with views of Bowness, the Bow River, and the mountains. Descend to the valley floor and hike the paved Bow River pathway through Shouldice Park, a multi-use park with baseball and soccer fields, an arena, and batting cages in summer. Finish the trek with a short backtrack on familiar streets.

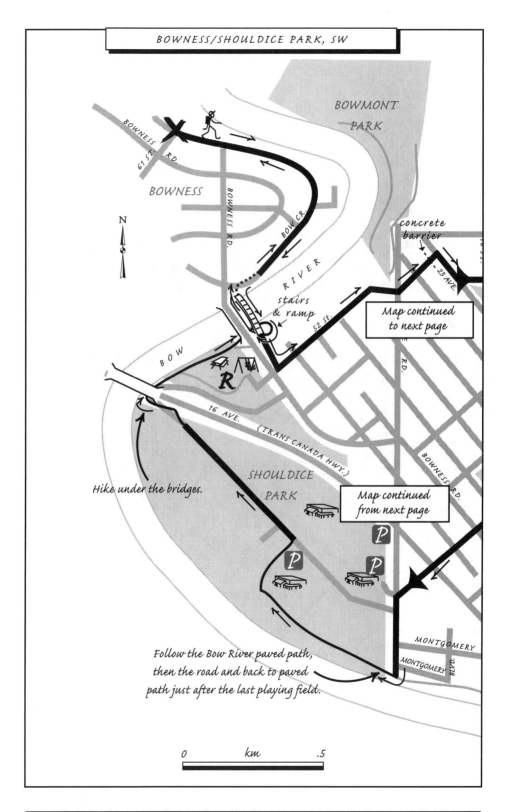

BOWMONT PARK

BOWNESS RD.

61 ST.

BOWNESS RD.

BOWNESS

N

BOW CR.

RIVER

concrete barrier

23 AVE.

stairs & ramp

52 St.

Map continued to next page

BOW

R

16 AVE.

(TRANS CANADA HWY.)

SHOULDICE PARK

Hike under the bridges.

Map continued from next page

P

P

P

BOWNESS RD.

MONTGOMERY BLVD.

MONTGOMERY

Follow the Bow River paved path, then the road and back to paved path just after the last playing field.

0   km   .5

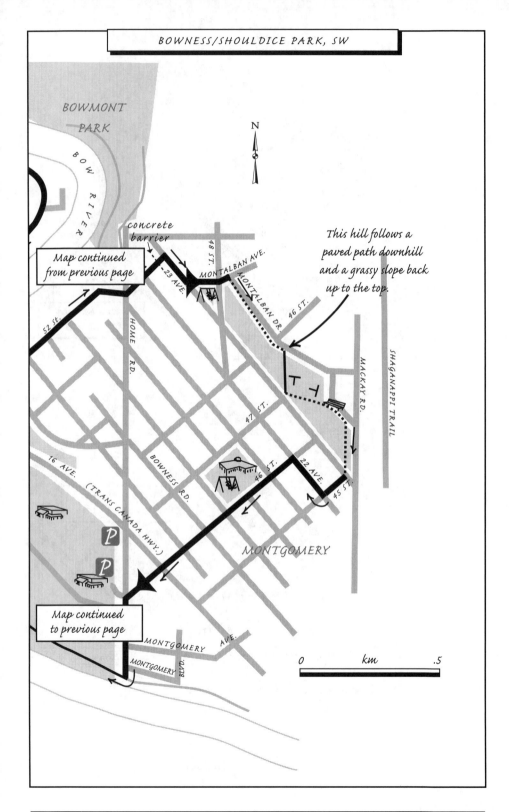

BOWMONT
PARK

B O W   R I V E R

N

concrete
barrier

Map continued
from previous page

48 ST.

MONTALBAN AVE.

MONTALBAN DR.

23 AVE.

This hill follows a
paved path downhill
and a grassy slope back
up to the top.

46 ST.

52 ST.

HOME RD.

MACKAY RD.

SHAGANAPPI TRAIL

47 ST.

16 AVE. (TRANS CANADA HWY.)

BOWNESS RD.

46 ST.

22 AVE.

45 ST.

P

P

MONTGOMERY

Map continued
to previous page

MONTGOMERY AVE.

MONTGOMERY BLVD.

MONTGOMERY

0   km   .5

Confederation Park/ Nose Hill, NW

Categories: *neighbourhood, nature*
Approximate Distance: *10 kilometres*
Approximate Time: *2.5 hours*
Degree of Difficulty: *easy and flat through Confederation Park and neighbourhoods; moderate on Nose Hill, with hills and hill-training options*
Parking: *two official parking lots on 10 Street between 24 Avenue and Rosehill Drive*
Facilities: *playgrounds; bathroom on 30 Avenue (open year round)*

Hike at a Glance

For the indecisive hiker, this route has a bit of everything: paved paths through mani-cured parks, sidewalks through established neighbourhoods, a taste of the prairies, some hill climbing on Nose Hill, expansive city views, and a cemetery walk to finish things off. Tired yet? Even though you can hike this route year round, it is at its best in the summer and fall when the trees are in full leaf, the neighbourhood gardens are blooming, and the Nose Hill prairie grasses are long and lush.

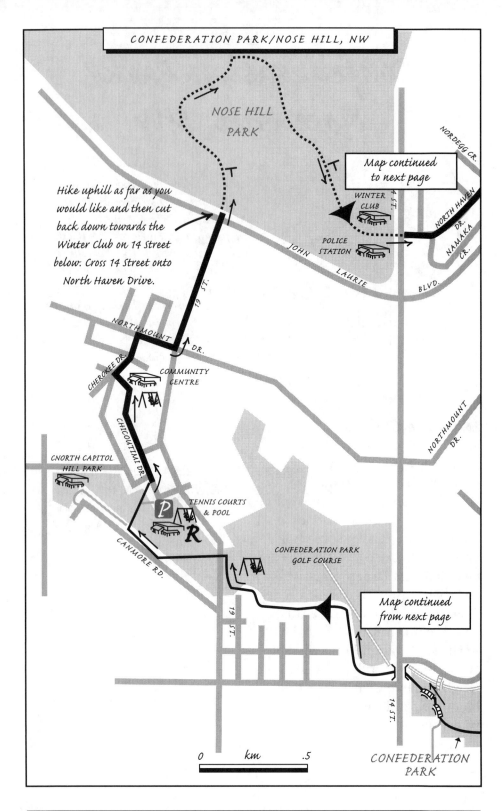

CONFEDERATION PARK/NOSE HILL, NW

NOSE HILL PARK

Map continued to next page

WINTER CLUB

4 ST.

POLICE STATION

NORDEGG CR.

NORTH HAVEN DR.

NAMAKA CR.

BLVD.

JOHN LAURIE

Hike uphill as far as you would like and then cut back down towards the Winter Club on 14 Street below. Cross 14 Street onto North Haven Drive.

19 ST.

NORTHMOUNT DR.

CHEROKEE DR.

COMMUNITY CENTRE

CHICOUTIMI DR.

NORTHMOUNT DR.

CNORTH CAPITOL HILL PARK

P

TENNIS COURTS & POOL

R

CANMORE RD.

CONFEDERATION PARK GOLF COURSE

Map continued from next page

19 ST.

14 ST.

CONFEDERATION PARK

0   km   .5

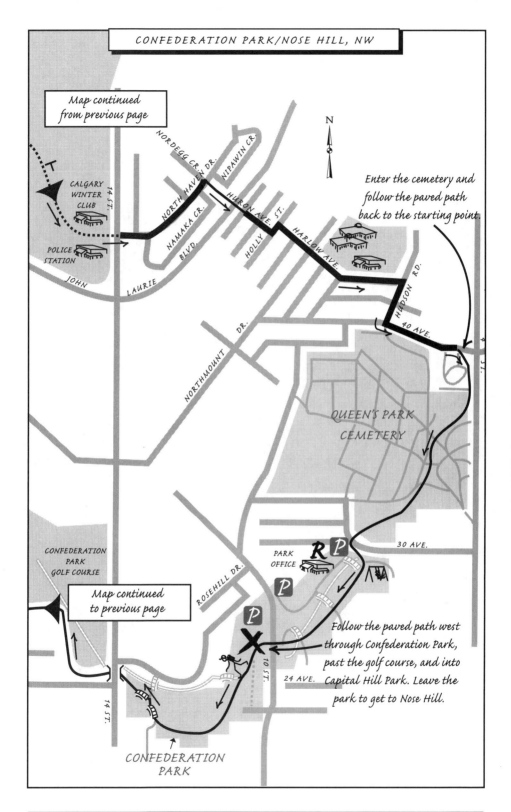

Map continued from previous page

N

CALGARY WINTER CLUB

POLICE STATION

NORDEGG CR.

NIPAWIN CR.

14 ST.

NORTH HAVEN DR.

NAMAKA CR.

HURON AVE. ST.

HOLLY

HARLOW AVE.

Enter the cemetery and follow the paved path back to the starting point.

HUDSON RD.

40 AVE.

4 ST.

JOHN

LAURIE

NORTHMOUNT DR.

QUEEN'S PARK CEMETERY

CONFEDERATION PARK GOLF COURSE

Map continued to previous page

ROSEHILL DR.

PARK OFFICE

R P

P

P

30 AVE.

Follow the paved path west through Confederation Park, past the golf course, and into Capital Hill Park. Leave the park to get to Nose Hill.

10 ST.

24 AVE.

14 ST.

CONFEDERATION PARK

Briar Hill/ Parkdale, NW

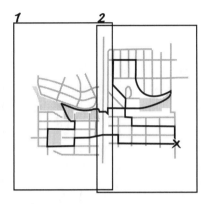

Category: *neighbourhood*
Approximate Distance: *6 kilometres*
Approximate Time: *1.5 hours*
Degree of Difficulty: *easy, mainly flat with one hill climb and many optional trail-training hills*
Parking: *street parking at the corner of 4 Avenue and 19 Street, and on side streets*
Facilities: *none*

Hike at a Glance

Briar Hill is a pleasant neighbourhood to explore. A perfectly placed green space makes for great climbing and a picture-postcard view of Calgary's downtown core. One noisy walkover above Crowchild Trail is a necessary evil that leads to Parkdale. The homes along the escarpment occupy prime real estate, with a park close by and views in all directions. The escarpment trails have sweating potential if you are so inclined. A flat walk through the streets of Parkdale and West Hillhurst gives you time to think, redecorate your home, in your mind at least, or collect some landscaping ideas.

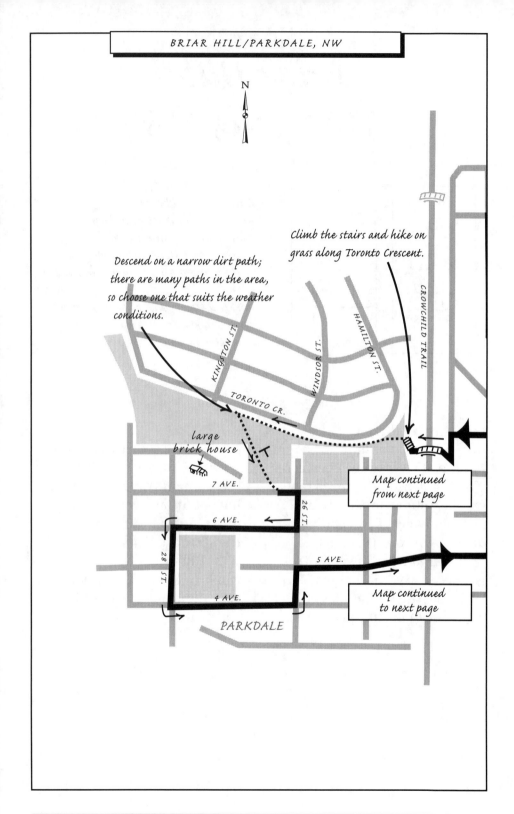

N

Climb the stairs and hike on grass along Toronto Crescent.

Descend on a narrow dirt path; there are many paths in the area, so choose one that suits the weather conditions.

CROWCHILD TRAIL

KINGSTON ST.

WINDSOR ST.

HAMILTON ST.

TORONTO CR.

large brick house

7 AVE.

26 ST.

Map continued from next page

6 AVE.

28 ST.

5 AVE.

Map continued to next page

4 AVE.

PARKDALE

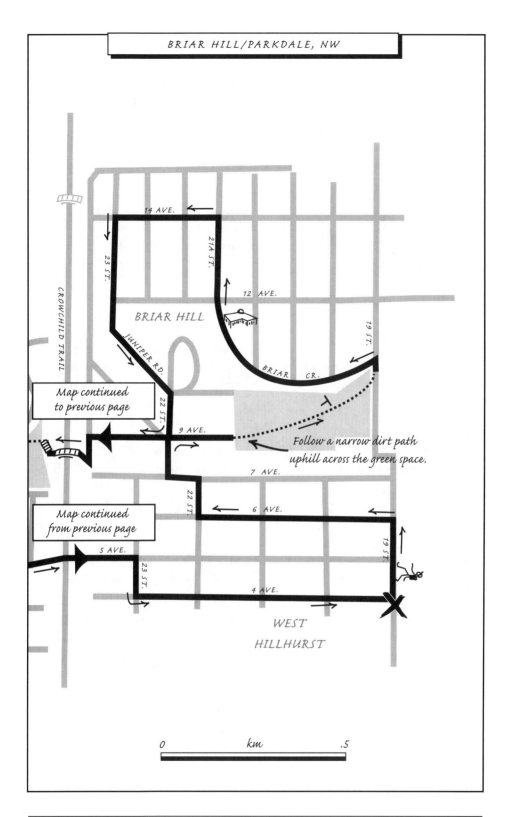

BRIAR HILL

14 AVE.

21A ST.

23 ST.

12 AVE.

CROWCHILD TRAIL

JUNIPER RD.

22 ST.

19 ST.

BRIAR CR.

Map continued
to previous page

9 AVE.

Follow a narrow dirt path
uphill across the green space.

7 AVE.

22 ST.

6 AVE.

19 ST.

Map continued
from previous page

5 AVE.

23 ST.

4 AVE.

WEST

HILLHURST

0   km   .5

McHugh Bluff/ Prince's Island, NW

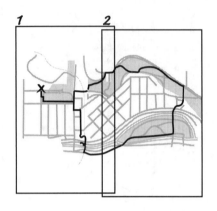

Categories: *trail training, park/neighbourhood, coffee shop*
Approximate Distance: *7 kilometres*
Approximate Time: *1.5 hours*
Degree of Difficulty: *moderate, with some challenging hills and stairs; many trail training options*
Parking: *street parking at the intersection of 12 Street and 8 Avenue; official parking lot at Riley Park*
Facilities: *bathroom (open from May to September); wading pool; playgrounds; picnic tables*

Hike at a Glance

Hike year round along Riley Park pathways, Sunnyside sidewalks, and the stairs and hills of McHugh Bluff. The bluff at the edge of Crescent Heights is a hill climber's dream come true. Not only can you work up a great sweat, but when you stop to catch your breath you are also rewarded with impressive views. In the summer, the tourists flock to the top of the massive stairs across from Prince's Island to soak up views of the Calgary skyline, Rocky Mountains, and Bow River. Since they have usually driven to the top of the bluff,

visitors are always impressed when a hiker achieves the summit. To impress them even more, tell them you have 129 times to go until you've climbed the elevation of Everest, and then hope they leave soon so you don't have to make good on this statement. Cross the river and loop back through Prince's Island and Sunnyside, back to Riley Park.

Seasonal Highlights/ Cautions

Summer: Enjoy the colourful rock gardens in Burns Memorial Park.

Fitness Tip

TRAIL TRAINING

If you want an alternative to the Crescent Heights stairs, try the paved path that gradually climbs the escarpment. Gradual hills are perfect for quadriceps training. These big muscles in the front of your leg are used constantly when alpine skiing or hill-climbing on a bike. Build quad strength by walking backwards for twenty steps and then forwards for another twenty steps. Keep alternating direction until you reach the top. The bigger the steps you take, the tougher the workout.

Shopping Tip

BEST BAGELS

Add weight to your backpack with some authentic Montreal-style bagels from Wayne's Bagels in Kensington. Baked fresh daily in their wood-fired oven, there are many types to choose from. Try multigrain, sesame, or blueberry. Grab a tub of flavoured cream cheese and you are all set for a picnic on Prince's Island. Location: 328-10 Street NW

HEARTLAND CAFÉ

Kensington is coffee shop central. Heartland Café is off the beaten path and is my favourite for its great atmosphere. After this hike you will appreciate their freshly baked goods, healthy soups and salads, and more substantial meals (just in case you did climb the stairs 130 times!). Location: 940-2 Avenue NW

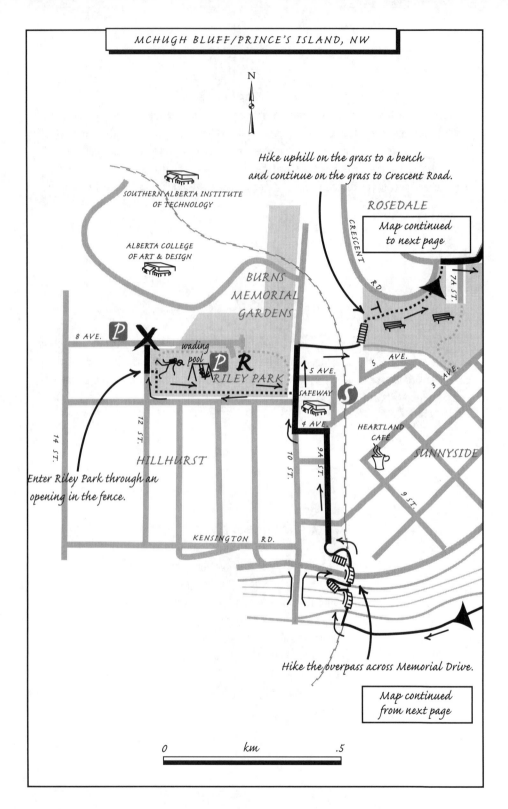

N

Hike uphill on the grass to a bench
and continue on the grass to Crescent Road.

SOUTHERN ALBERTA INSTITUTE
OF TECHNOLOGY

ALBERTA COLLEGE
OF ART & DESIGN

ROSEDALE

CRESCENT RD.

Map continued
to next page

7A ST.

BURNS
MEMORIAL
GARDENS

8 AVE.

wading
pool

RILEY PARK

5 AVE.

5 AVE.

3 AVE.

SAFEWAY

4 AVE.

HEARTLAND
CAFÉ

SUNNYSIDE

12 ST.

14 ST.

HILLHURST

10 ST.

9A ST.

9 ST.

Enter Riley Park through an
opening in the fence.

KENSINGTON RD.

Hike the overpass across Memorial Drive.

Map continued
from next page

0   km   .5

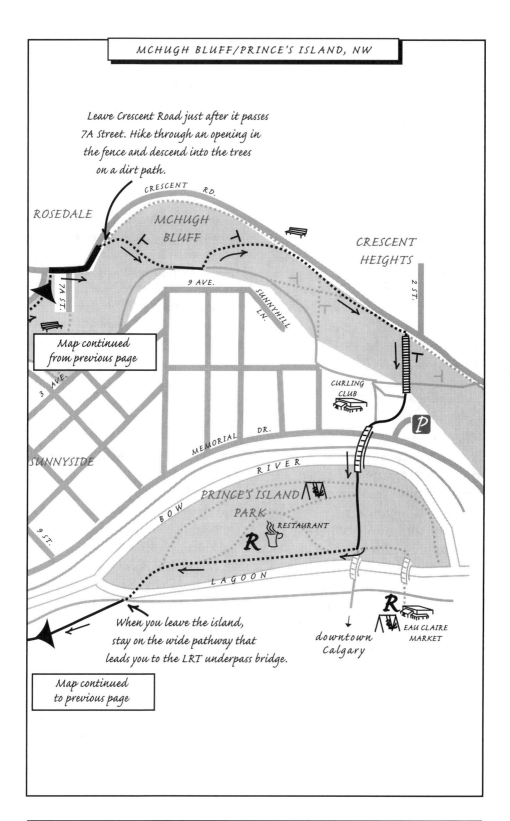

Leave Crescent Road just after it passes
7A Street. Hike through an opening in
the fence and descend into the trees
on a dirt path.

CRESCENT RD.

ROSEDALE

MCHUGH
BLUFF

CRESCENT
HEIGHTS

9 AVE.

SUNNYHILL LN.

7A ST.

2 ST.

Map continued
from previous page

3 AVE.

CURLING
CLUB

MEMORIAL DR.

SUNNYSIDE

BOW RIVER

PRINCE'S ISLAND
PARK

RESTAURANT

R

9 ST.

LAGOON

EAU CLAIRE
MARKET

downtown
Calgary

When you leave the island,
stay on the wide pathway that
leads you to the LRT underpass bridge.

Map continued
to previous page

Regal Terrace/ Sunnyside, NE/NW

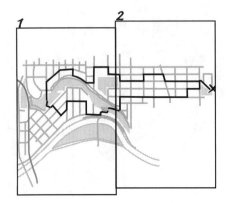

Categories: *neighbourhood, coffee shop*
Approximate Distance: *7 kilometres*
Approximate Time: *1.5 hours*
Degree of Difficulty: *easy, with a few hills; lots of stairs and hills for optional training*
Parking: *street parking at the corner of Regent Crescent and Radford Road*
Facilities: *none*

Hike at a Glance

Enjoy a pleasant sidewalk stroll along the tree-lined streets of three of Calgary's older neighbourhoods. Regal Terrace is a pleasant community where well-kept, modest homes host colourful gardens. In December, the Christmas lights are a treat in Crescent Heights, and the Bow River and city core views from the McHugh Bluff escarpment are camera worthy. Take a narrow dirt path down to Sunnyside, an eclectic neighbourhood whose charms come from an assortment of abodes that vary from walk-up apartment complexes to renovated older homes and even some handyman delights. Its proximity to the city core and the funky district of Kensington keeps Sunnyside young and vibrant. Enjoy the stairs or paved-path climb back to Crescent Heights while returning to the car.

Seasonal Highlights/ Cautions

Summer: Enjoy the gardens along this route.
Fall: Large trees line the streets on this trek; in September, they are full of fall colour.

LINA'S ITALIAN MARKET AND CAPPUCCINO BAR

Have a real Italian experience when you visit Lina's for your post-hike indulgence. Steaming hot cappuccinos mix well with homemade orange pistachio or chocolate paradise biscotti. There is lots to choose from at the dessert bar, but why not try the Sicilian cannoli or chocolate-dipped cannoli for something a little different? If it's lunch you want, then order an individual-sized focaccia pizza, or buy a pizza for a picnic lunch on the trail. It's worth doing an extra set of stairs on your hike if you plan on stopping at Lina's! Location: 2202 Centre Street NE

Enjoy Bow River and downtown Calgary views as you catch your breath on this Crescent Heights hillside.

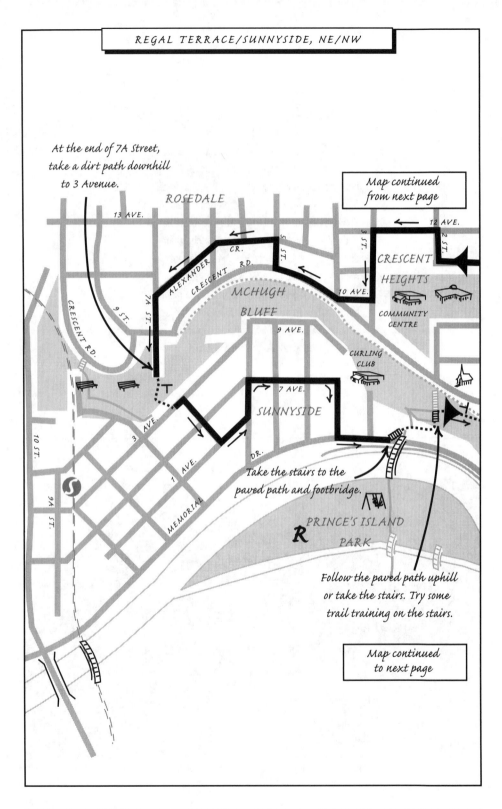

At the end of 7A Street,
take a dirt path downhill
to 3 Avenue.

ROSEDALE

13 AVE.

Map continued
from next page

12 AVE.

CRESCENT

HEIGHTS

3 ST.

5 ST.

CR.

ALEXANDER

CRESCENT RD.

MCHUGH

BLUFF

10 AVE.

COMMUNITY
CENTRE

9 ST.

7A ST.

CRESCENT RD.

9 AVE.

CURLING
CLUB

3 AVE.

SUNNYSIDE

7 AVE.

10 ST.

9A ST.

1 AVE.

DR.

MEMORIAL

Take the stairs to the
paved path and footbridge.

R PRINCE'S ISLAND

PARK

Follow the paved path uphill
or take the stairs. Try some
trail training on the stairs.

Map continued
to next page

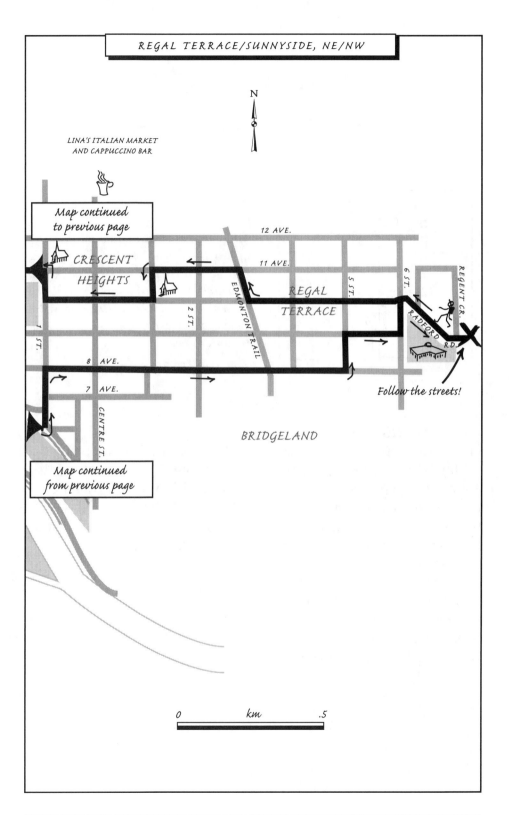

N

LINA'S ITALIAN MARKET
AND CAPPUCCINO BAR

Map continued
to previous page

CRESCENT
HEIGHTS

12 AVE.

11 AVE.

REGAL
TERRACE

5 ST.

6 ST.

REGENT CR.

RADFORD RD.

EDMONTON TRAIL

2 ST.

1 ST.

8 AVE.

7 AVE.

CENTRE ST.

BRIDGELAND

Follow the streets!

Map continued
from previous page

0   km   .5

Bridgeland/ Bow River, NE

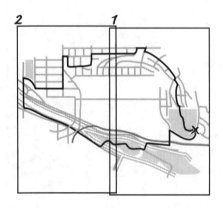

Categories: *neighbourhood, trail training, historic*
Approximate Distance: *7 kilometres*
Approximate Time: *1.75 hours*
Degree of Difficulty: *easy, with hill options*
Parking: *street parking in an obvious pull-off on the south side of St. George's Drive, just west of the first zoo parking lot; official zoo parking lots*
Facilities: *none*

Hike at a Glance

Climb to the top of Tom Campbell's Hill for a view of the hike to come. Too bad the zoo doesn't graze its exotic animals here anymore—it would be fun to see a camel off-leash area. Bridgeland is a culturally diverse community. Its streets are quite un-Calgarian, criss-crossing haphazardly on the hillside and adding character to the area. Italian, Russian, Ukranian, and German influences linger, especially on 1 Street, where some tasty treats await. But you have to climb the stairs first! The landmark copper-domed Ukrainian Catholic Church marks a set of stairs that will determine your post-hike indulgence. You want dessert too?

Climb the next hill with thoughts of tiramisu. The views are worth the climb. Finally, cross the river, hike past Chinatown, cross St. Patrick's Island, and return to the zoo parking lot.

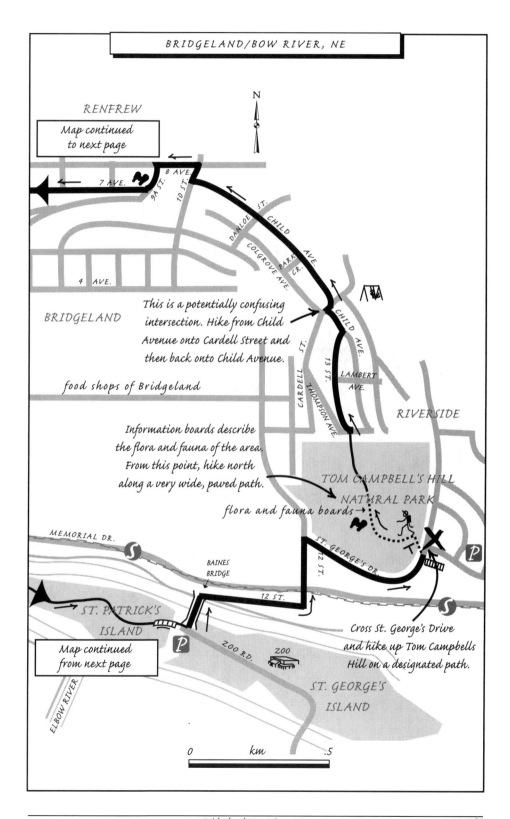

RENFREW

Map continued
to next page

7 AVE.   8 AVE.

9 ST.   10 ST.

DANLOE ST.

CHILD AVE.

COLGROVE AVE.

PARK CR.

4 AVE.

BRIDGELAND

This is a potentially confusing
intersection. Hike from Child
Avenue onto Cardell Street and
then back onto Child Avenue.

food shops of Bridgeland

CARDELL ST.

THOMPSON AVE.

CHILD AVE.

13 ST.

LAMBERT AVE.

RIVERSIDE

Information boards describe
the flora and fauna of the area.
From this point, hike north
along a very wide, paved path.

TOM CAMPBELL'S HILL
NATURAL PARK

flora and fauna boards →

MEMORIAL DR.

BAINES
BRIDGE

ST. GEORGE'S DR.

12 ST.

P

ST. PATRICK'S
ISLAND

12 ST.

Map continued
from next page

P

ZOO RD.   ZOO

Cross St. George's Drive
and hike up Tom Campbells
Hill on a designated path.

ELBOW RIVER

ST. GEORGE'S
ISLAND

0   km   .5

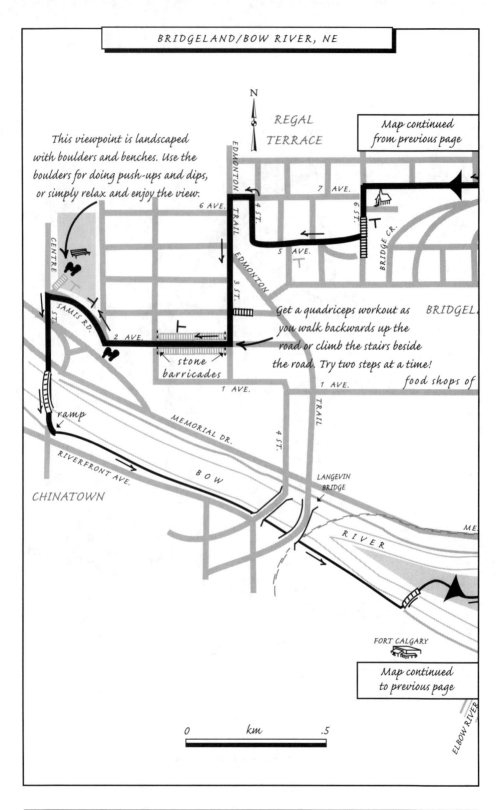

N

REGAL TERRACE

Map continued from previous page

This viewpoint is landscaped with boulders and benches. Use the boulders for doing push-ups and dips, or simply relax and enjoy the view.

7 AVE.

6 AVE.

EDMONTON TRAIL

4 ST.

5 ST.

BRIDGE CR.

CENTRE

5 AVE.

EDMONTON 3 ST.

SAMIS RD.

BRIDGEL.

Get a quadriceps workout as you walk backwards up the road or climb the stairs beside the road. Try two steps at a time!

2 AVE.

stone barricades

1 AVE.

1 AVE.

4 ST.

TRAIL

food shops of

ramp

MEMORIAL DR.

RIVERFRONT AVE.

BOW

CHINATOWN

LANGEVIN BRIDGE

ME

RIVER

FORT CALGARY

Map continued to previous page

ELBOW RIVER

0   km   .5

Strathcona Ravine, SW

Categories: *park/neighbourhood, coffee shop*
Approximate Distance: *4 kilometres*
Approximate Time: *0.75 hours*
Degree of Difficulty: *easy and flat;*
optional training hills
Parking: *street parking on Christie Park Manor*
Facilities: *none*

Hike at a Glance

This short walk combines a jaunt through the suburbs with a peaceful stroll through a tree-canopied ravine. A combination of paved, shale, and narrow dirt paths leads you into the Strathcona Ravine, which is dominated by aspen, balsam poplar, and low-lying shrubs. In the fall, the foliage colours are vibrant and the solitude is a welcome treat. This trek is a tribute to the City of Calgary's park planning and effective integration of wild park areas into neighbourhood settings.

Seasonal Highlights/ Cautions

Spring: The west end of the ravine can be icy and muddy.
Fall: The ravine is an oasis of colour and solitude.

SUNTERRA MARKET CAFÉ

Combine your grocery shopping with a cappuccino and freshly baked muffin, cookie, or piece of cake at Sunterra Market. There is also a full menu of lunches and suppers available if you need something a bit more substantial. This is a great place to stock up on tasty breads, cheeses, and fresh produce. Location: 1851 Sirocco Drive SW

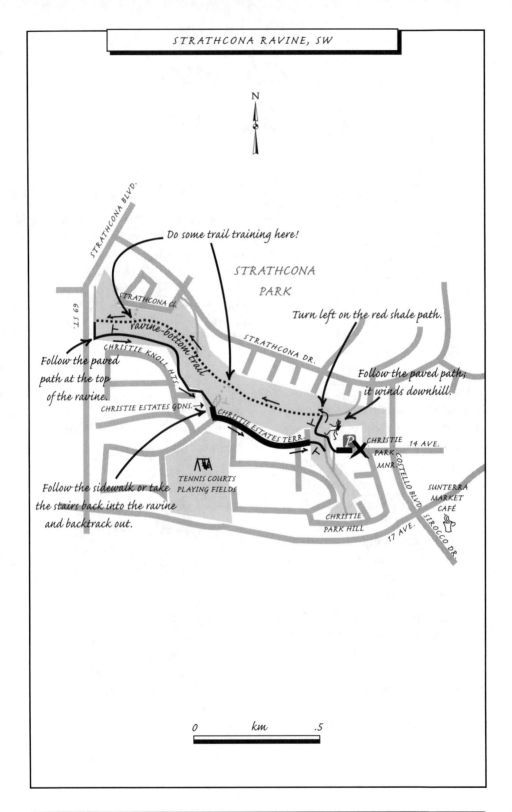

N

Do some trail training here!

STRATHCONA
PARK

Turn left on the red shale path.

STRATHCONA BLVD.

STRATHCONA cl.

69 ST.

ravine-bottom trail

STRATHCONA DR.

CHRISTIE KNOLL HTS.

Follow the paved
path at the top
of the ravine.

Follow the paved path;
it winds downhill.

CHRISTIE ESTATES GDNS.

CHRISTIE ESTATES TERR.

CHRISTIE
PARK
MNR

14 AVE.

COSTELLO BLVD.

SIROCCO DR.

TENNIS COURTS
PLAYING FIELDS

SUNTERRA
MARKET
CAFÉ

Follow the sidewalk or take
the stairs back into the ravine
and backtrack out.

CHRISTIE
PARK HILL

17 AVE.

0   km   .5

Edworthy Park, SW

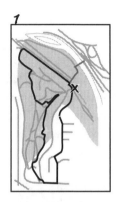

Categories: *trail training, nature, coffee shop (see neighbouring Hike 19 for description and location)*
Approximate Distance: *5 kilometres*
Approximate Time: *1.25 hours*
Degree of Difficulty: *moderate, with some steep hills and many hill-training options*
Parking: *from Bow Trail, turn north on 45 Street, west on Spruce Drive, and then follow Edworthy Park Street downhill to the parking lot*
Facilities: *bathroom (open from May to September); playground; picnic tables; barbecue pits*

Hike at a Glance

A flat trek beside the train tracks warms you up before a dirt path leads you uphill into the trees. Continue on a combination of wide and narrow dirt paths through a wide-open, tail-wagging, off-leash area. Lactic-acid-building, hill-training options follow. The steep hills can be avoided if you would rather enjoy views than cough up a lung. I often meet hikers in training for trekking in Nepal on the steep hill overlooking the south Edworthy parking lot. Bring your poles and save your knees if you plan on multiple ascents. A quiet, wooded escarpment trail leads to the neighbourhood of Wildwood as you loop back to your car.

Seasonal Highlights/ Cautions

Winter and Spring: The trails can be muddy and icy throughout winter and into spring.

History Notes

PEMMICAN

The cliffs and steep slopes of this area made it a good spot for the Plains Indians to stampede buffalo. One bull could supply up to 225 kilograms of meat. This meat was an ingredient of pemmican, a mixture of dried meat, berries, and fatty bone marrow that was stored in buffalo-skin bags. Pemmican was the main winter food source for the Plains Indians. European explorers also enjoyed it as a nutritious and long-lasting part of their diet.

SANDSTONE CITY

In the late 1800s, four stone quarries, known as the Bow Bank Quarries and located in the Edworthy Park area, supplied most of the building material for downtown Calgary. Sandstone became the building material of choice after a fire destroyed fourteen wooden buildings in downtown Calgary in 1886. As a result of the fire, the City of Calgary passed an ordinance stating that certain buildings, such as hotels, had to be constructed of material more permanent than wood.

BRICKBURN

Shortly after the turn of the century, the popularity of sandstone as a building material began to decline. In 1905, Brickburn was established, a bustling community that housed the workers and families of the Calgary Pressed Brick and Sandstone Co. Brick was a low-cost alternative to sandstone and at its peak, the company was producing eighty thousand bricks daily, from fifteen kilns. In 1914, the plant was one of four on the continent capable of creating top-quality enamelled brick. Today this area is the most westerly point of Edworthy Park.

Fitness Tip

BURNING MUSCLES

Climbing steep hills can make your muscles burn. As the intensity of an activity increases and you stop breathing comfortably, your activity becomes anaerobic or "without oxygen." A byproduct of anaerobic exercise is an accumulation of lactic acid in your muscles. The muscle burn that you feel when exercising is caused by the lactic acid accumulation and means your muscles are tired. Slow down or stop your activity when you feel the burn. Fitness levels determine lactic acid thresholds, so the fitter you are, the more you can climb before you feel the burn.

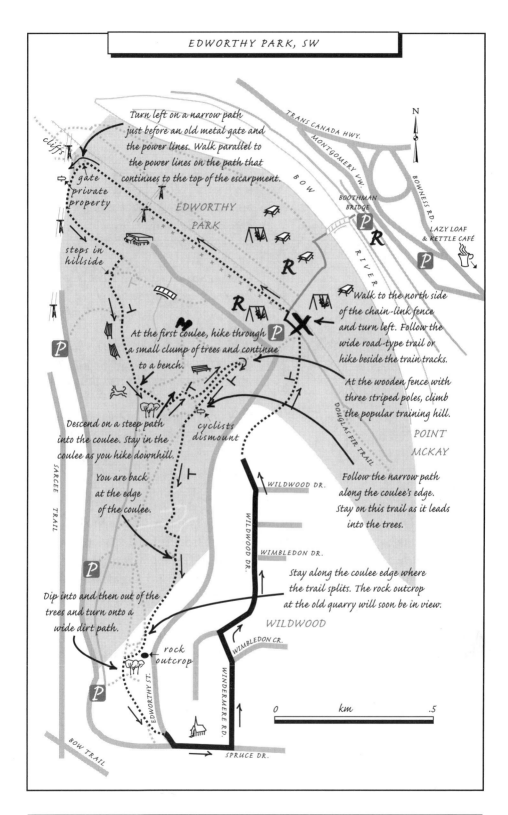

Turn left on a narrow path just before an old metal gate and the power lines. Walk parallel to the power lines on the path that continues to the top of the escarpment.

cliffs

gate
private
property

EDWORTHY
PARK

steps in
hillside

TRANS CANADA HWY.

MONTGOMERY VW.

B O W

BOOTHMAN
BRIDGE

R I V E R

LAZY LOAF
& KETTLE CAFÉ

N

BOWNESS RD.

R

Walk to the north side of the chain-link fence and turn left. Follow the wide road-type trail or hike beside the train tracks.

At the first coulee, hike through a small clump of trees and continue to a bench.

At the wooden fence with three striped poles, climb the popular training hill.

POINT
MCKAY

Descend on a steep path into the coulee. Stay in the coulee as you hike downhill.

cyclists
dismount

Follow the narrow path along the coulee's edge. Stay on this trail as it leads into the trees.

You are back at the edge of the coulee.

SARCEE

TRAIL

DOUGLAS FIR TRAIL

WILDWOOD DR.

WILDWOOD DR.

WIMBLEDON DR.

Stay along the coulee edge where the trail splits. The rock outcrop at the old quarry will soon be in view.

WILDWOOD

Dip into and then out of the trees and turn onto a wide dirt path.

rock
outcrop

WIMBLEDON CR.

0   km   .5

EDWORTHY ST.

WINDERMERE RD.

BOW TRAIL

SPRUCE DR.

Douglas Fir Trail, SW

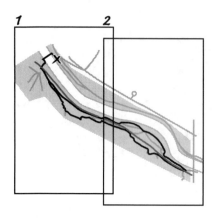

Categories: *trail training, nature, coffee shop, kids*

Approximate Distance: *8 kilometres*

Approximate Time: *2 hours*

Degree of Difficulty: *challenging on the way out, easy return*

Parking/North: *at the intersection of Bowness Road and Shaganappi Trail, turn onto Montgomery View and continue to the official parking areas*

Parking/South: *follow 45 Street north from Bow Trail to Spruce Drive; turn west and follow the signs along the winding gravel road to the parking lot*

Facilities: *bathroom (open year round); playgrounds; picnic tables; concession (open in summer); barbecue pits*

Hike at a Glance

This lovely trail is one of Calgary's best kept secrets! If you want to get away from the city without travelling far, then hike the Douglas Fir Trail. Turn off the paved path onto the signed trail. A combination of stairs, bridges, and dirt paths leads you through a rare stand of 400-year-old Douglas fir trees, with circumferences up to 2 metres around. Climb to enjoy views of the Bow River and then descend until you turn back at the halfway point to follow the flat, paved path along the Bow River. In the fall, great horned owls like to fly low across the path at dusk. Tip your head back and watch for them in the open grassy areas of this trek.

Seasonal Highlights/ Cautions

Winter and Spring: The trail is treacherous due to the presence of ice flows on the paved path and on steep sections of the stairs; the ice sometimes stays until the end of May.

History Notes

WILDWOOD SLIDE

A sign that states "Slide Area, No Stopping" marks the spot where a landslide swept twenty-eight rail cars off the tracks in 1956. The instability of the slope is due partly to the number of natural springs in the area. Slide activity was also increased with the development of the communities of Spruce Cliff and Wildwood. There are safety measures in place to prevent another slide in this area; however, these have no effect on adjacent slopes. As you hike the trail, watch for trees and telephone poles that show signs of tilting and bridges that are being displaced.

LOWERY GARDENS

John Lawrey arrived in Calgary in 1881. A green-thumbed farmer from England, he is credited with changing the area west of town from frontier to a settled, agrricultural community. Today Lowery Gardens, the land that bears his name at the east end of Douglas Fir Trail, is spelled incorrectly due to the many misspellings found on official documents. It is one of the most productive bird-watching areas in Calgary.

Fitness Tip

MOUNTAINEER STEP

Stay off your toes if you want to be able to breathe comfortably when climbing hills! Instead, practise the "mountaineer" or "rest" step. Take a step uphill, straighten the forward leg by letting your heel come back to the ground, and then take your next step uphill. If the hill is really steep, you may want to count 1 second between steps. This endurance technique lets you relax your calf muscles and breathe easily, so you have lots of energy for the long haul. Slow and steady is the key to enjoyment and endurance!

LAZY LOAF AND KETTLE CAFÉ

The Lazy Loaf and Kettle Café is a great place to replenish lost calories with homemade baked goods and hearty lunches. My personal favourites are the cinnamon buns, which are as big as your head. While you are there, buy a loaf of kettle bread to take home. It's delicious and it's healthy! Drive or walk east on Memorial Drive and turn left into Parkdale Crescent.
Location: 8 Parkdale Crescent NW

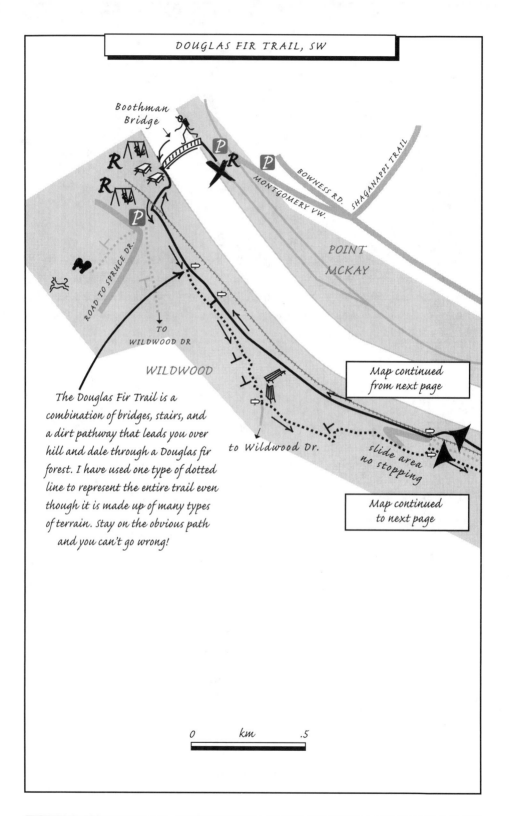

Boothman Bridge

ROAD TO SPRUCE DR.

TO WILDWOOD DR

WILDWOOD

BOWNESS RD.

MONTGOMERY VW.

SHAGANAPPI TRAIL

POINT MCKAY

Map continued from next page

to Wildwood Dr.

slide area no stopping

Map continued to next page

The Douglas Fir Trail is a combination of bridges, stairs, and a dirt pathway that leads you over hill and dale through a Douglas fir forest. I have used one type of dotted line to represent the entire trail even though it is made up of many types of terrain. Stay on the obvious path and you can't go wrong!

0   km   .5

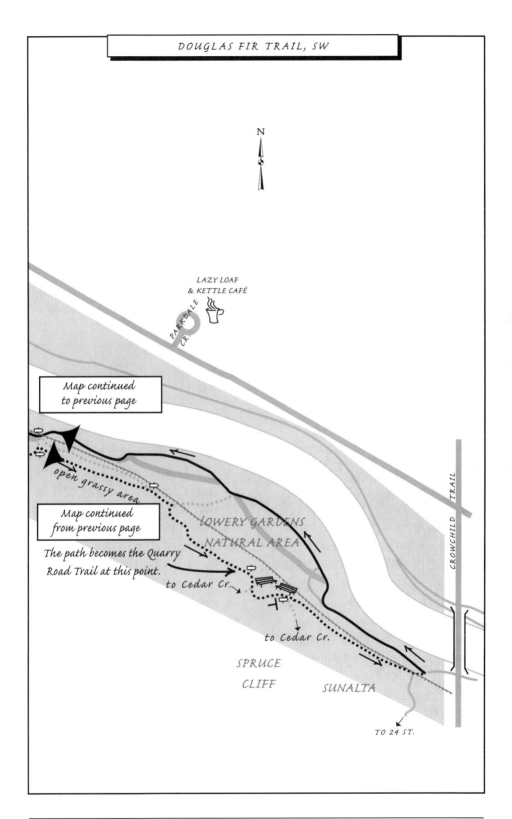

N

LAZY LOAF
& KETTLE CAFÉ

PARKDALE
CR.

Map continued
to previous page

open grassy area

Map continued
from previous page

The path becomes the Quarry
Road Trail at this point.

LOWERY GARDENS
NATURAL AREA

to Cedar Cr.

to Cedar Cr.

SPRUCE
CLIFF

SUNALTA

CROWCHILD TRAIL

TO 24 ST.

Bow River/ Scarboro, SW

Categories: *neighbourhood*

Approximate Distance: *7 kilometres*

Approximate Time: *1.5 hours*

Degree of Difficulty: *easy and mostly flat; one long hill is good for trail-training*

Parking: *follow Pumphouse Road to the Pumphouse Theatre; park on the road or in the parking lot near the theatre*

Facilities: *none*

Hike at a Glance

If urban hikers "bag communities" like mountain hikers "bag peaks," then this is an outing worth bragging about. Travel through five neighbourhoods on this down-to-earth, pleasant stroll. Begin with paved paths along the Bow River, which are followed by a long, gradual climb to the neighbourhood of Sunalta. The remainder of the trek follows sidewalks through quiet and not-so-quiet neighbourhoods. Well-kept, modest homes in Glengarry give way to renovated abodes from the 1950s and brand new in-fills in Knob Hill. Bankview combines high-density apartment complexes with homes from the early 1900s that have been reno-

vated by funky, young urbanites. Cross 17 Avenue and enter Scarboro, a well-to-do area with cozy homes on tree-lined streets full of character. A large sandstone school marks the hidden path that short-cuts back to Sunalta.

This route is nice at any time of year, but it is especially colourful in the summer, when gardens are full, and in the fall, when hedges turn burnt orange and red.

Seasonal Highlights/ Cautions

Winter: In December, thousands of Christmas lights decorate the homes in these neighbourhoods.

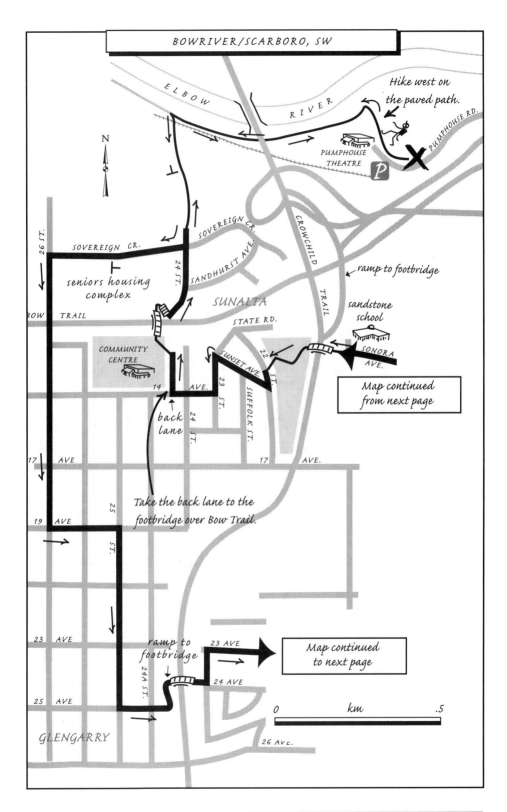

Hike west on the paved path.

ELBOW RIVER

PUMPHOUSE RD.

PUMPHOUSE THEATRE

P

N

SOVEREIGN CR.

SOVEREIGN CR.

SANDHURST AVE.

24 ST.

26 ST.

seniors housing complex

BOW TRAIL

SUNALTA

CROWCHILD TRAIL

ramp to footbridge

sandstone school

STATE RD.

SONORA AVE.

22 ST.

SUNSET AVE.

23 ST.

Map continued from next page

COMMUNITY CENTRE

14 AVE.

24 ST.

SUFFOLK ST.

back lane

17 AVE

17 AVE.

Take the back lane to the footbridge over Bow Trail.

19 AVE

25 ST.

23 AVE

ramp to footbridge

23 AVE

24A ST.

24 AVE

Map continued to next page

25 AVE

0   km   .5

GLENGARRY

26 AVE.

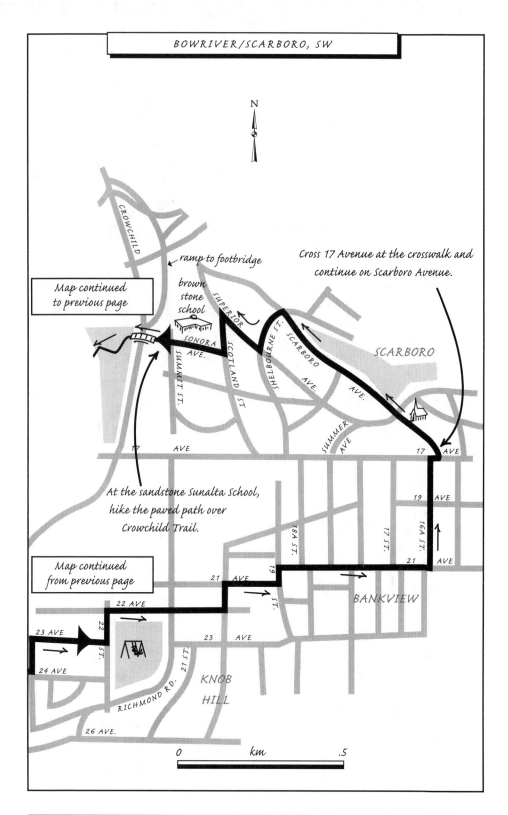

N

CROWCHILD

ramp to footbridge

Cross 17 Avenue at the crosswalk and
continue on Scarboro Avenue.

brown
stone
school

Map continued
to previous page

SUPERIOR

SONORA
AVE.

SCOTLAND ST

SUMMIT ST.

SHELBOURNE ST.

SCARBORO
AVE.

SCARBORO
AVE.

SCARBORO

17   AVE

SUMMER
AVE

17   AVE

At the sandstone Sunalta School,
hike the paved path over
Crowchild Trail.

19   AVE

16A ST.

17 ST.

18A ST.

21   AVE

Map continued
from previous page

21   AVE

19   ST.

21   ST.

BANKVIEW

22 AVE

22
ST.

23   AVE

KNOB
HILL

23 AVE

RICHMOND RD.   21 ST.

24 AVE

26 AVE.

0   km   .5

Elbow Park/ Mount Royal, SW

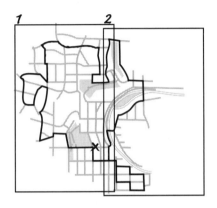

Categories: *neighbourhood, trail training, historic*
Approximate Distance: *6 kilometres*
Approximate Time: *1.25 hours*
Degree of Difficulty: *easy, with a few hills; optional stairs for trail training*
Parking: *street parking on 34 Avenue near the Elbow Park Community Centre*
Facilities: *bathrooms in community centre; playground; outdoor skating rink; tennis courts*

Hike at a Glance

Follow sidewalks along hilly, tree-lined streets and explore one of Calgary's oldest and most affluent neighbourhoods. Comprising a combination of unique character homes from the early 1900s and interesting modern dwellings, Mount Royal makes me sigh, gasp, and wonder how many guide-books I would have to sell to live in such a stunning community. It is filled with beautiful gardens in the summer and wonderful light displays at Christmas. In summer you will also see lots of half-ton trucks carrying landscape designers, yard maintenance specialists, and general contrac-tors. They make their fortune here and you can enjoy the results of their work on this colourful trek.

Seasonal Highlights/ Cautions

Summer: There are gardens galore to enjoy on this hike.
Winter: Take pleasure from the colourful Christmas lights in December.

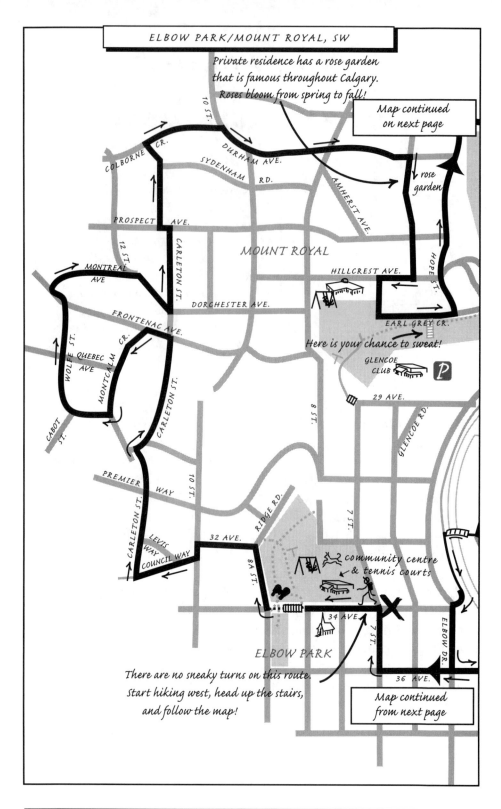

ELBOW PARK/MOUNT ROYAL, SW

Private residence has a rose garden
that is famous throughout Calgary.
Roses bloom from spring to fall!

Map continued
on next page

rose
garden

10 ST.

COLBORNE CR.

DURHAM AVE.

SYDENHAM RD.

AMHERST AVE.

PROSPECT AVE.

CARLETON ST.

12 ST.

MOUNT ROYAL

HILLCREST AVE.

HOPE ST.

MONTREAL AVE

FRONTENAC AVE.

DORCHESTER AVE.

WOLFE ST.

QUEBEC AVE

MONTCALM CR.

MONTCALM

CARLETON ST.

EARL GREY CR.

Here is your chance to sweat!

GLENCOE CLUB

29 AVE.

8 ST.

GLENCOE RD.

CABOT ST.

PREMIER WAY

10 ST.

RIDGE RD.

7 ST.

CARLETON ST.

LEVIS WAY

COUNCIL WAY

32 AVE.

8A ST.

community centre
& tennis courts

ELBOW DR.

ELBOW PARK

34 AVE.

7 ST.

There are no sneaky turns on this route.
Start hiking west, head up the stairs,
and follow the map!

Map continued
from next page

36 AVE.

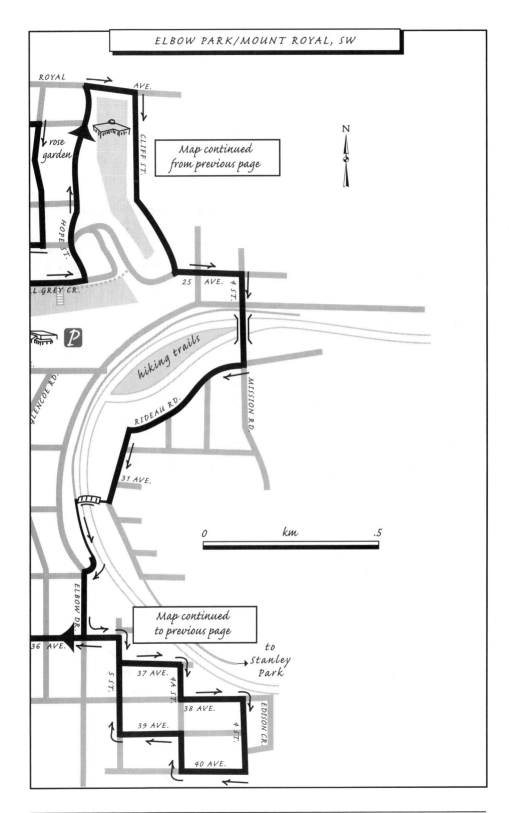

ELBOW PARK/MOUNT ROYAL, SW

ROYAL AVE.

rose garden

HOPE ST.

CLIFF ST.

Map continued
from previous page

N

 L GREY CR.

P

hiking trails

25 AVE.

4 ST.

MISSION RD.

GLENCOE RD.

RIDEAU RD.

31 AVE.

0   km   .5

ELBOW DR.

Map continued
to previous page

to
Stanley
Park

36 AVE.

5 ST.

37 AVE.

4A ST.

38 AVE.

EDISON CR.

4 ST.

39 AVE.

40 AVE.

Ramsay/ Inglewood, SE

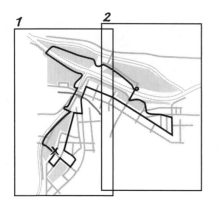

Categories: *neighbourhood, historic*
Approximate Distance: *6 kilometres*
Approximate Time: *1.25 hours*
Degree of Difficulty: *easy with some hill options and one mandatory set of stairs*
Parking: *street parking on Scotsman's Hill at the corner of Salisbury Street and Burns Avenue*
Facilities: *none*

Hike at a Glance

Hike tree-lined streets with small, stucco homes and tidy yards, and enjoy the feel of a multi-generational neighbourhood. Homes here date back to the late 1800s and the sense of community is strong. Old-timers enjoy green grassy yards with a few flowers for colour, whereas young families and the artsy set landscape with rock gardens and stone walkways. After enjoying the awesome views from the top of Scotsman's Hill, descend along roads that go this way and that, and have poetic names like Bison Path (a road no bigger than a path). Closer to the Bow River, bay windows and verandahs, decorative widow's walks on rooftops, and fine woodwork make this an architecturally interesting jaunt. Cross the river and follow paved paths past the Calgary Zoo, which has a great Christmas light display in December; then cross a wooded island before looping past Fort Calgary. Watch for great horned owls at dusk on the hike back along the Elbow River. A long set of well-lit stairs leads you back to the top of Scotsman's Hill.

History Note

WHAT'S IN A NAME?

The name Scotsman's Hill comes from the large numbers of people who watch the Calgary Exhibition and Stampede activities from the hill to avoid paying the Stampede admission charge.

Entertainment Note

CULTURED HIKING

Inglewood is full of antique shops, warehouse-turned-art studios, small, independent theatre companies, cool cafés, and ethnically diverse restaurants and stores. Have a cultured hike!

Visit the Village Hearth and Terrace Café for the Dinner and Drag Queen show on Saturday nights.

Loose Moose Theatre Company has improvisational theatre and theatresports, or check with the Green Fools Theatre Company for mask shows and more.

Scotsman's Hill offers impressive views while you work up a sweat on the stairs.

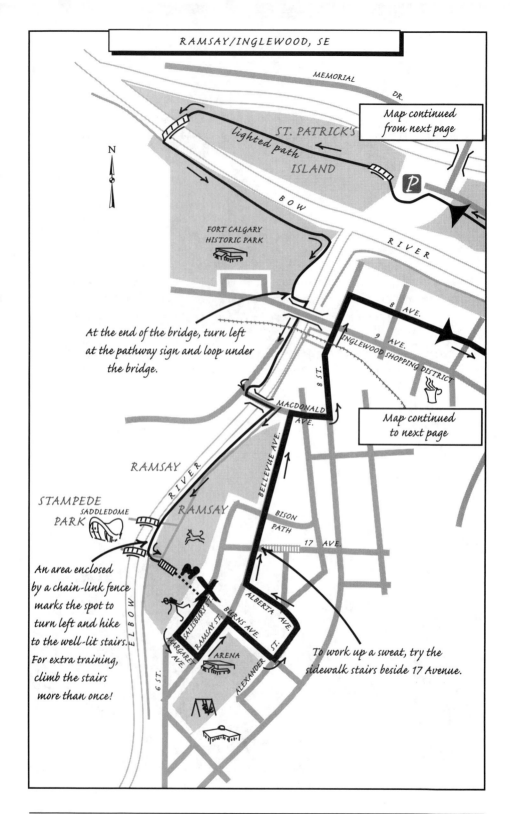

N

Map continued
from next page

MEMORIAL DR.

ST. PATRICK'S
ISLAND

lighted path

BOW

RIVER

FORT CALGARY
HISTORIC PARK

8 AVE.

9 AVE.

INGLEWOOD SHOPPING DISTRICT

At the end of the bridge, turn left
at the pathway sign and loop under
the bridge.

8 ST.

MACDONALD
AVE.

Map continued
to next page

RAMSAY

RIVER

BELLEVUE AVE.

STAMPEDE
PARK

SADDLEDOME

RAMSAY

BISON
PATH

17 AVE.

An area enclosed
by a chain-link fence
marks the spot to
turn left and hike
to the well-lit stairs.
For extra training,
climb the stairs
more than once!

ELBOW

ALBERTA AVE.

SALISBURY ST.

RAMSAY ST.

BURNS AVE.

MARGARET AVE.

ARENA

6 ST.

ALEXANDER ST.

To work up a sweat, try the
sidewalk stairs beside 17 Avenue.

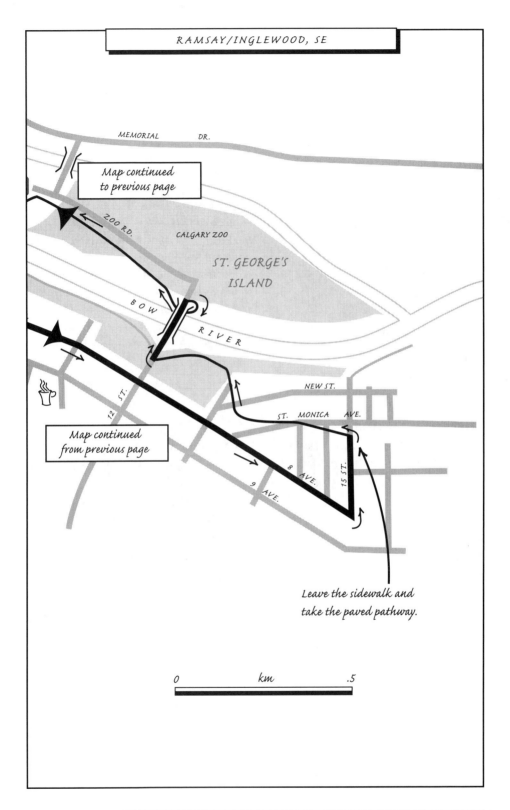

MEMORIAL DR.

Map continued
to previous page

ZOO RD.

CALGARY ZOO

ST. GEORGE'S
ISLAND

BOW RIVER

Map continued
from previous page

NEW ST.

ST. MONICA AVE.

12 ST.

8 AVE.

9 AVE.

15 ST.

Leave the sidewalk and
take the paved pathway.

0   km   .5

Inglewood Bird Sanctuary, SE

Category: *nature*
Approximate Distance: *4 kilometres*
Approximate Time: *0.75 hours*
Degree of Difficulty: *easy and flat*
Parking: *official parking lot near the end of 9 Avenue at Sanctuary Road*
Facilities: *visitor centre (open in summer from May long weekend to October long weekend, Monday to Sunday, 10:00 AM to 5:00 PM; open in winter from Tuesday to Sunday, 10:00 AM to 4:00 PM); bathrooms (open during visitor centre hours)*

Hike at a Glance

This 32-hectare wildlife reserve is a feathered favourite. Stroll along paved and shale paths beside the Bow River while keeping a keen eye open for rare birds. More than 270 species of birds have been seen here, 53 of which nest on site and the rest of which are migratory. For all you non-birding types, this is a great place to unwind, learn about birds from the visitor centre staff, and watch binocular-clad birders do their stuff.

Seasonal Bird Sightings

Winter: Chickadees are friendly visitors throughout winter when thousands of ducks and geese spend time on the open-water lagoon and Bow River.

Spring: A variety of waterfowl begin to arrive in March, followed by shorebirds in May, while songbirds add music to your hike in May and June.

Summer: Watch for pelicans and cormorants throughout July and August. Colourful Baltimore orioles, yellow warblers, flycatchers, and eastern kingbirds are a common sight in the warm months.

Autumn: August and September are busy months when a variety of warbler species pay a visit to the sanctuary.

RARE BIRD SIGHTINGS

Spring and fall are the best times for spotting rare birds at the sanctuary. Call the Bird Alert Hotline (237-8821), which keeps an update of recent rare bird sightings.

History Note

COLONEL JAMES WALKER: 1846-1936

You can thank the Walker family for your trek today since it was Colonel James Walker's son who turned the Walker property into what is now the Inglewood Bird Sanctuary. In 1975, James Walker was named Calgary's Citizen of the Century. Throughout his varied career he spent time with the North West Mounted Police defending Forts Battleford, Walsh, Pelly, and Calgary. Known for his honesty and fairness, he excelled in such roles as Indian Agent and negotiator, earning him the trust of aboriginals and settlers alike. He achieved financial success when he established the Bow River Mills, a sawmill that supplied timber to settlers and railway ties to the Canadian Pacific Railway. From laying the first sidewalk to providing the city with natural gas illumination from his own well, Walker's contributions to Calgary were many, which made him a standout over the other three thousand nominees to become Calgary's Citizen of the Century.

Nature Note

BIRD FACTS

Are dinosaurs dead? Look around, those chickadees are probably the descendants of a Mesozoic monster. Indeed, if it wasn't for the preserved feathers, the oldest known bird (Archaeopteryx) would have been mistaken for a dinosaur.

Birds never pee. To conserve water, birds secret urea crystals, the white stuff that goes splat.

Crows eat their own weight in food every day, consuming from eight to ten full meals.

Hummingbirds eat about every 10 minutes, slurping down twice the weight of their tiny body in nectar every day.

A bird's heart beats four hundred times per minute while resting and up to one thousand beats per minute while flying.

Oddly, most birds have little or no sense of smell. One of the favourite foods of the great horned owl is the skunk!

Many species of birds clean their feathers with live ants.

Air sacs may make up one-fifth of the body volume of a bird.

A bird's normal body temperature is usually 7 to 8 degrees hotter than a human's. Up to three-quarters of the air a bird breathes is used just for cooling, since they are unable to sweat.

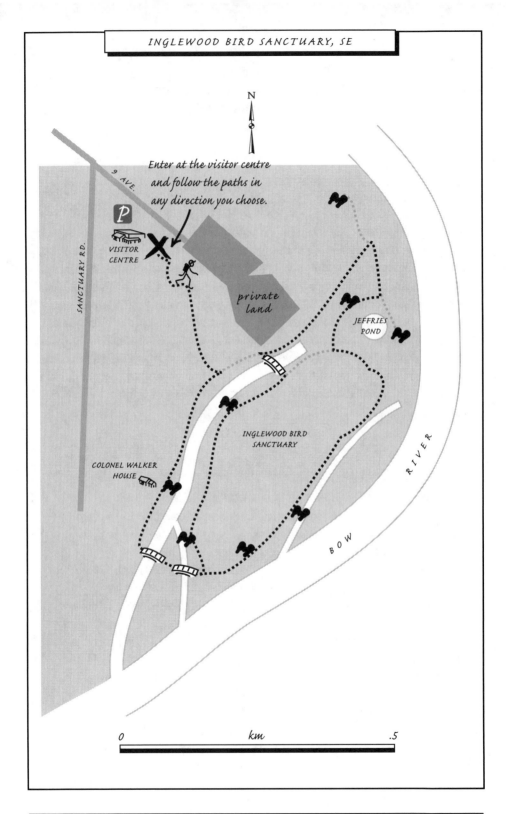

N

Enter at the visitor centre
and follow the paths in
any direction you choose.

9 AVE.

SANCTUARY RD.

P

VISITOR
CENTRE

private
land

JEFFRIES
POND

INGLEWOOD BIRD
SANCTUARY

COLONEL WALKER
HOUSE

BOW RIVER

0   km   .5

Roxboro/ Stanley Park, SW

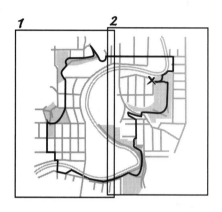

Categories: *park/neighbourhood, trail training*
Approximate Distance: *7 kilometres*
Approximate Time: *1.5 hours*
Degree of Difficulty: *moderate, with some challenging hills; many stair and hill-training options*
Parking: *street parking in the vicinity of Roxboro Road and Roxboro Glen Road*
Facilities: *bathrooms (open from May to September); picnic tables; barbecue pits; swimming pool (open in summer); concession (open in summer); tennis courts*

Hike at a Glance

Wonderful mini-parks are hidden throughout established neighbourhoods in Calgary. Roxboro Natural Park is one such secret gem. A treed dirt pathway climbs to the top of the escarpment where expansive views of Mission, Connaught, and downtown Calgary towers are the reward. Native grasses, shrubs, and flowers line the path, and in spring, the musky scent of wolf willows is almost overwhelming! From dirt path to sidewalks, up stairs and along the river pathways, you will travel through Parkhill, Riverdale, Elbow Park, and Roxboro. Filled with large character homes, wonderful gardens, and great Christmas light displays, these neighbourhoods are pleasing to the eye but hard on the pocketbook. Riverdale homes are some of the most expensive in Calgary. Make sure to work up a sweat on the Glencoe stairs before looping back through the trendy Mission shopping area to Roxboro.

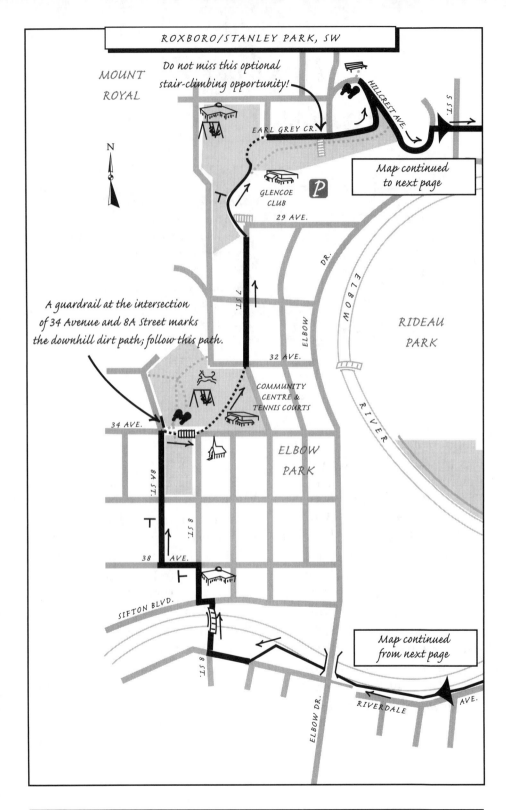

ROXBORO/STANLEY PARK, SW

MOUNT ROYAL

Do not miss this optional stair-climbing opportunity!

HILLCREST AVE.

5 ST.

EARL GREY CR.

N

Map continued to next page

GLENCOE CLUB

29 AVE.

DR.

ELBOW

RIDEAU PARK

A guardrail at the intersection of 34 Avenue and 8A Street marks the downhill dirt path; follow this path.

7 ST.

ELBOW

32 AVE.

COMMUNITY CENTRE & TENNIS COURTS

RIVER

34 AVE.

ELBOW PARK

8A ST.

8 ST.

38 AVE.

SIEFTON BLVD.

Map continued from next page

8 ST.

RIVERDALE AVE.

ELBOW DR.

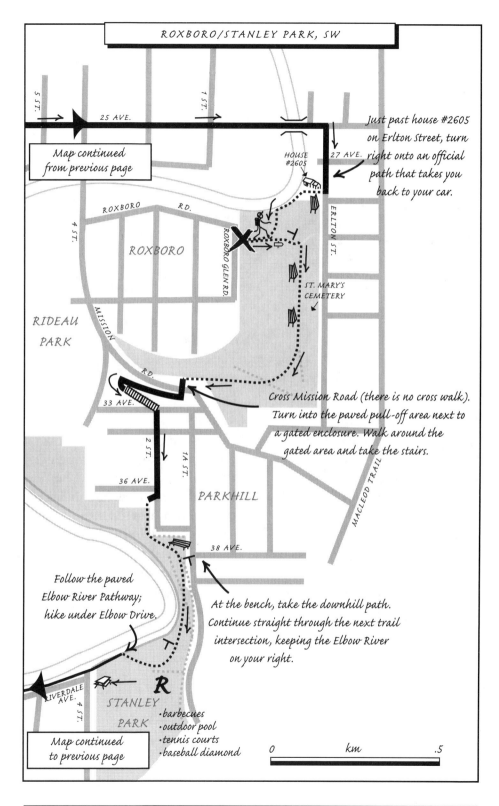

5 ST.

25 AVE.

1 ST.

Just past house #2605
on Erlton Street, turn
right onto an official
path that takes you
back to your car.

HOUSE
#2605

27 AVE.

ERLTON ST.

Map continued
from previous page

ROXBORO   RD.

4 ST.

ROXBORO

ROXBORO GLEN RD.

St. MARY'S
CEMETERY

RIDEAU

PARK

MISSION

RD.

33 AVE.

Cross Mission Road (there is no cross walk).
Turn into the paved pull-off area next to
a gated enclosure. Walk around the
gated area and take the stairs.

2 ST.

1A ST.

36 AVE.

PARKHILL

MACLEOD TRAIL

38 AVE.

Follow the paved
Elbow River Pathway;
hike under Elbow Drive.

At the bench, take the downhill path.
Continue straight through the next trail
intersection, keeping the Elbow River
on your right.

R

RIVERDALE
AVE.

4 ST.

STANLEY

PARK

· barbecues
· outdoor pool
· tennis courts
· baseball diamond

Map continued
to previous page

0   km   .5

Reader Rock Garden/ Elbow River, SW

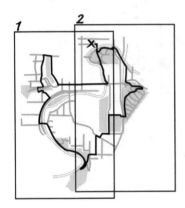

Category: *park/neighbourhood, coffee shop*
Approximate Distance: *7 kilometres*
Approximate Time: *1.5 hours*
Degree of Difficulty: *moderate, mainly flat with optional hills and stairs throughout*
Parking: *street parking on 19 Avenue near 1 Street (2 hour free parking zone)*
Facilities: *none; bathrooms at Lindsay Park Sports Complex*

Hike at a Glance

Hike along paved paths through Lindsay Park to red shale paths and old roads that lead to the Reader Rock Garden. Know worldwide in its prime for its unique and diverse plant collection, this rock garden was once a work of art and is still a great place for Calgary gardeners to draw inspiration. Take some photos before hiking along the edge of Union Cemetery. Next, take a jaunt through Erlton. Following sidewalks through Parkhill, hike past unique homes, such as the old brick school that has been converted into condos and colourful in-fills with lots of character. Enjoy views of the Elbow River valley before descending into Stanley Park. Follow the Elbow River to upscale Rideau and then into Mount Royal.

WILLIAM READER

As you walk through the Reader Rock Garden, imagine that in 1913, the site was nothing more than a dusty, barren land. Thanks to William Reader, an Englishman who brought his love of gardening to Calgary in 1908, the site was transformed. In April 1913, Reader became the parks superintendent for Calgary and during his 29-year career, he helped develop many of Calgary's parks, cemeteries, and civic nurseries. Between 1922 and 1929, thousands of tons of boulders, originating from Banff to Drumheller, were brought to the site to create an alpine rock garden. Reader's passion for gardening led him to collect plants from around the world. He introduced many of these into the rock gardens and at one time, up to 850 varieties of seeds were documented in the Reader Rock Garden. Reader taught Calgarians that it is possible to have a beautiful garden in Calgary, despite our tough growing conditions.

Nature Note

CHINOOKS

When the moist air from the west coast hits the mountains, warm winds called Chinooks descend on Calgary. Chinook means "snow eater," but could mean "snow plow" in Calgary since we depend on it to clear snow-filled side streets. Calgarians love to brag to relatives and friends back east about the huge temperature changes during some Chinooks. "It went from −20°C to +20°C in one day" they will report to snow-weary friends. Chinook thaws make gardening here a challenge, which is why William Reader's rock garden was so impressive in its prime. Trees and plants can be tricked into budding by warm winds in January, only to be frozen during the next deep freeze. It's the price we pay for our trademark blue skies and warm winds.

MANUEL LATRUWE BELGIAN PATISSERIE & BREAD SHOP

If you are feeling low on calories, then this is the place for you. Real butter and real cream make the croissants, chocolate buns, and miniature dessert creations at Manuel Latruwe taste truly decadent. For lunch, try a quiche and then grab a loaf of bread to enjoy later. If you would like to delay your sweet tooth gratification, buy a tub of homemade ice cream for a future indulgence. Location: 1333-1 Street SE (on Macleod Trail S, beside the Bernard Callebaut building)

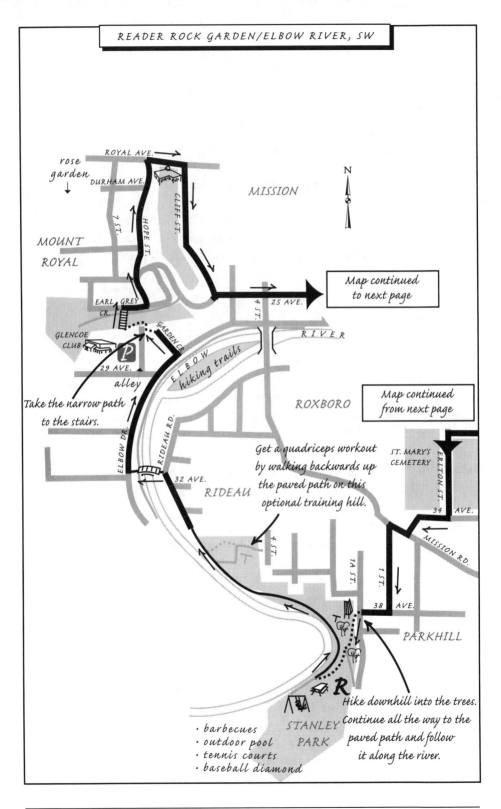

rose garden

ROYAL AVE.

DURHAM AVE.

MISSION

MOUNT ROYAL

7 ST.

HOPE ST.

CLIFF ST.

N

Map continued to next page

EARL GREY CR.

4 ST.

25 AVE.

GLENCOE CLUB

29 AVE.

P

GARDEN CR.

alley

ELBOW RIVER

hiking trails

Take the narrow path to the stairs.

ELBOW DR.

RIDEAU RD.

32 AVE.

RIDEAU

ROXBORO

Map continued from next page

ST. MARY'S CEMETERY

ERLTON ST.

34 AVE.

Get a quadriceps workout by walking backwards up the paved path on this optional training hill.

4 ST.

MISSION RD.

1A ST.

1 ST.

38 AVE.

PARKHILL

R

Hike downhill into the trees. Continue all the way to the paved path and follow it along the river.

· barbecues
· outdoor pool
· tennis courts
· baseball diamond

STANLEY PARK

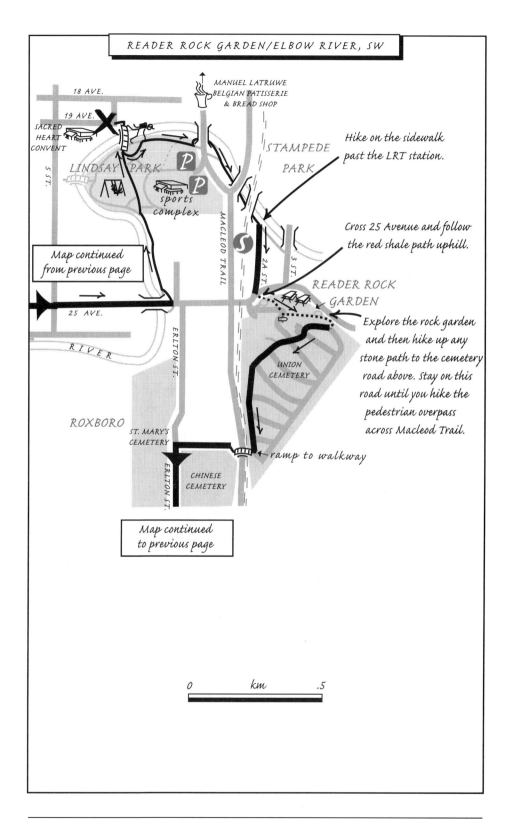

18 AVE.

19 AVE.

SACRED
HEART
CONVENT

5 ST.

LINDSAY PARK

P

P

sports
complex

MANUEL LATRUWE
BELGIAN PATISSERIE
& BREAD SHOP

STAMPEDE
PARK

MACLEOD TRAIL

2A ST.

3 ST.

Hike on the sidewalk
past the LRT station.

Cross 25 Avenue and follow
the red shale path uphill.

READER ROCK
GARDEN

Explore the rock garden
and then hike up any
stone path to the cemetery
road above. Stay on this
road until you hike the
pedestrian overpass
across Macleod Trail.

Map continued
from previous page

25 AVE.

RIVER

ERLTON ST.

UNION
CEMETERY

ROXBORO

ST. MARY'S
CEMETERY

ERLTON ST.

CHINESE
CEMETERY

ramp to walkway

Map continued
to previous page

0   km   .5

Garrison Woods/ Marda Loop, SW

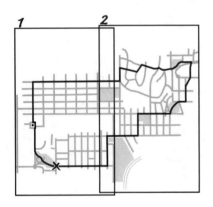

Category: *neighbourhood, coffee shop*
Approximate Distance: *8 kilometres*
Approximate Time: *1.75 hours*
Degree of Difficulty: *easy, with optional hills*
Parking: *street parking at the corner of 20 Street and 42 Avenue*
Facilities: *none*

Hike at a Glance

A hike that starts and ends at an ice cream shop is destined to become a favourite. This neighbourhood jaunt originates in the new development of Garrison Woods, a recent transformation of some of the former CFB Calgary Currie Barracks lands. A combination of single-family dwellings and high-end row houses lines streets named after World War I battles. Pass through the Marda Loop shopping district and into South Calgary. An up-and-coming neighbourhood, South Calgary gets pricier with every new in-fill that is developed. You can still see an old brown sandstone schoolhouse and many homes from the early 1950s that link the community to its past. Continue through Mount Royal and Elbow Park, two of Calgary's most character-filled neighbourhoods (not the people, the homes!). A short climb out of the river valley leads you to the homestretch through Altadore and back to the ice cream shop where your well-deserved treat awaits!

KAFFA CAFÉ AND SALSA HOUSE

Lots of primary colours on the walls make for an authentic Mexican feeling in this old-home-turned-funky coffee shop. Stop in after your trek for sweet-tooth treats or tasty tortillas and the special salsa of the day. The outdoor patio is a popular spot to relax and watch the world go by throughout the summer. Location: 2138-33 Avenue SW

BELL'S BOOKSTORE CAFÉ

Your post-perspiration pit stop is Bell's Bookstore Café. It's a great place to feed your soul with home-made goodies and to enjoy some great reading material. All the muffins are baked in small batches, so they are fresh throughout the day. The rhubarb muffins are fantastic! Location: 1515a-34 Avenue SW

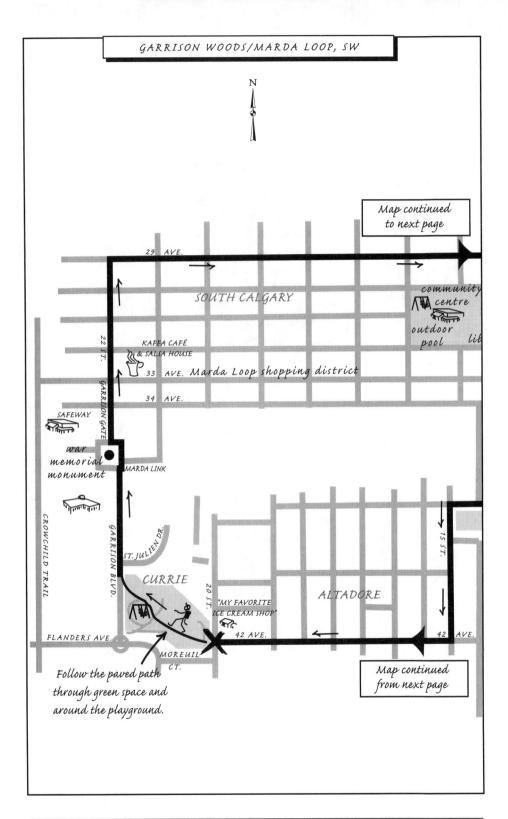

N

Map continued to next page

29 AVE.

SOUTH CALGARY

community centre

outdoor pool

lib

22 ST.

KAFFA CAFÉ & SALSA HOUSE

33 AVE. Marda Loop shopping district

34 AVE.

GARRISON GATE

SAFEWAY

war memorial monument

MARDA LINK

CROWCHILD TRAIL

GARRISON BLVD.

ST. JULIEN DR.

CURRIE

20 ST.

"MY FAVORITE ICE CREAM SHOP"

ALTADORE

15 ST.

FLANDERS AVE.

42 AVE.

42 AVE.

MOREUIL CT.

Follow the paved path through green space and around the playground.

Map continued from next page

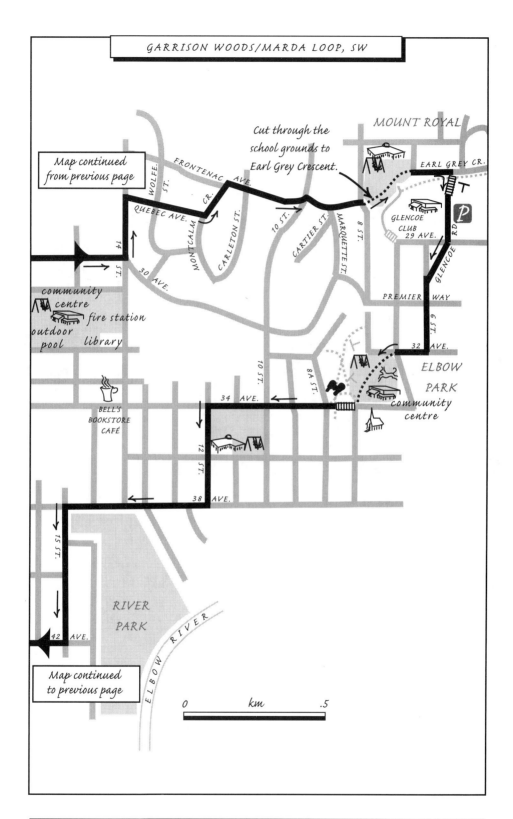

Cut through the school grounds to Earl Grey Crescent.

MOUNT ROYAL

EARL GREY CR.

FRONTENAC AVE.

WOLFE ST.

Map continued from previous page

QUEBEC AVE.

MONTCALM CR.

CARLETON ST.

10 ST.

CARTIER ST.

MARQUETTE ST.

8 ST.

GLENCOE CLUB

29 AVE.

GLENCOE RD.

14 ST.

30 AVE.

community centre
fire station
outdoor pool
library

PREMIER WAY

6 ST.

32 AVE.

ELBOW PARK

10 ST.

8A ST.

BELL'S BOOKSTORE CAFÉ

34 AVE.

community centre

12 ST.

38 AVE.

15 ST.

RIVER PARK

ELBOW RIVER

42 AVE.

Map continued to previous page

0   km   .5

Glenmore Dam/ Bel-Aire, SW

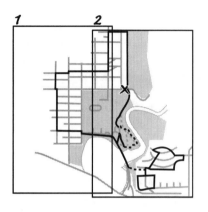

Category: *park/neighbourhood*
Approximate Distance: *7 kilometres*
Approximate Time: *1.5 hours*
Degree of Difficulty: *easy, with some optional hills*
Parking: *official parking lot at the intersection of 14A Street and 50 Avenue*
Facilities: *bathroom (portable)*

Hike at a Glance

Leave the paved path and follow single-track, dirt paths that dip down to the Elbow River below the Glenmore Dam. Only the locals know about this hidden gem of a hike. A peaceful wooded walk along the river leads to the dam. Climb a hill, cross the dam, and take a sidewalk stroll through the well-hidden and well-heeled neighbourhoods of Bel-Aire and Mayfair. A combination of gated estates and down-to-earth homes is tucked away on these quiet streets. Another community awaits you, so it's back over the dam to North Glenmore Park. Older homes with well-kept yards make for a pleasant jaunt before you head back through Altadore and along the edge of River Park.

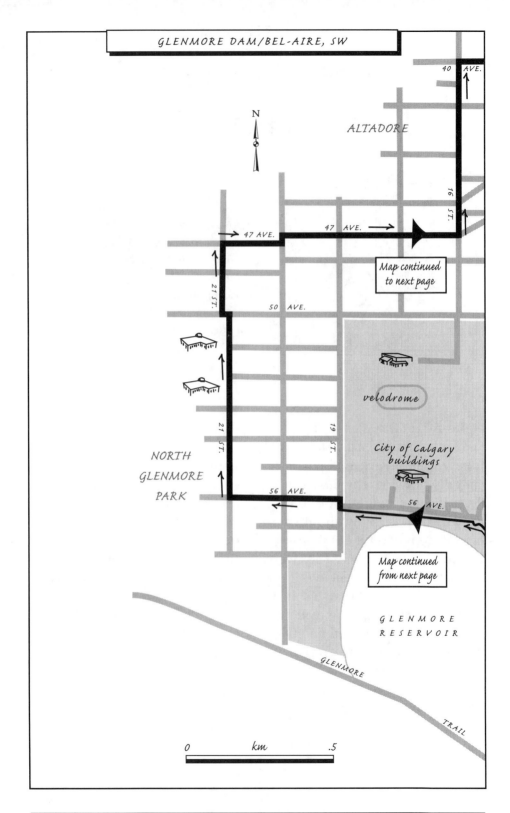

N

40 AVE.

ALTADORE

16 ST.

47 AVE.

47 AVE.

Map continued
to next page

21 ST.

50 AVE.

velodrome

21 ST.

19 ST.

City of Calgary
buildings

NORTH
GLENMORE
PARK

56 AVE.

56 AVE.

Map continued
from next page

GLENMORE
RESERVOIR

GLENMORE

TRAIL

0   km   .5

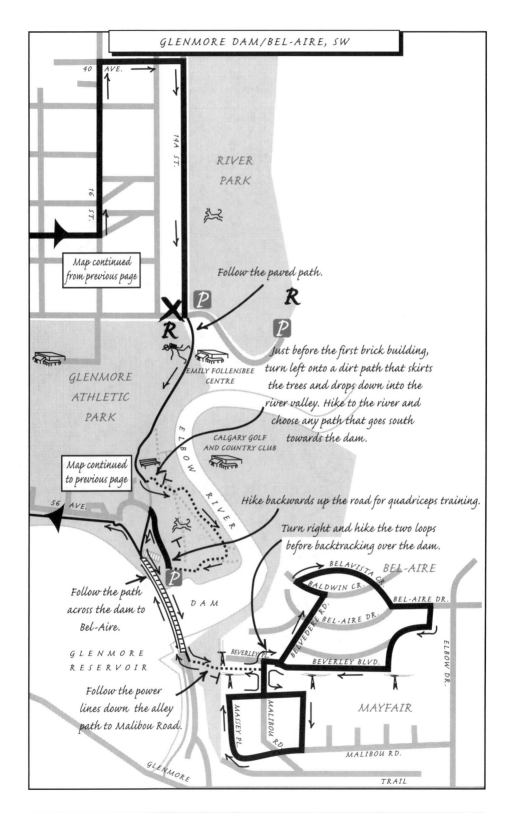

GLENMORE DAM/BEL-AIRE, SW

40 AVE.

14A ST.

16 ST.

RIVER PARK

Map continued from previous page

Follow the paved path.

Just before the first brick building, turn left onto a dirt path that skirts the trees and drops down into the river valley. Hike to the river and choose any path that goes south towards the dam.

GLENMORE ATHLETIC PARK

EMILY FOLLENSBEE CENTRE

ELBOW RIVER

CALGARY GOLF AND COUNTRY CLUB

Map continued to previous page

56 AVE.

Hike backwards up the road for quadriceps training.

Turn right and hike the two loops before backtracking over the dam.

BELAVISTA CR.
BALDWIN CR.
BELVEDERE RD.
BEL-AIRE DR.
BEL-AIRE DR.

BEL-AIRE

Follow the path across the dam to Bel-Aire.

DAM

BEVERLEY PL.
BEVERLEY BLVD.

ELBOW DR.

GLENMORE RESERVOIR

Follow the power lines down the alley path to Malibou Road.

MASSEY PL.
MALIBOU RD.

MAYFAIR

MALIBOU RD.

GLENMORE

TRAIL

Sandy Beach/ Mount Royal, SW

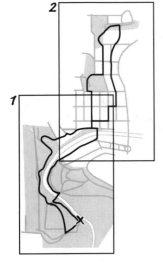

Categories: *park/neighbourhood, trail training, coffee shop*
Approximate Distance: *7 kilometres*
Approximate Time: *1.5 hours*
Degree of Difficulty: *moderate, with some challenging hills; many training options*
Parking: *at the intersection of 14A Street and 50 Avenue, take 50 Ave east past River Park and the Emily Follensbee Centre down to the Sandy Beach parking lot*
Facilities: *bathrooms (open from May to September); picnic tables; barbecue pits*

Hike at a Glance

From river valley to ridge-top, you will enjoy Elbow River views with a cityscape backdrop. My favourite time to hike here is the early morning, when the sky is blue and the songbirds are in full celebration. The route follows gravel paths through River Park, over footbridges and into some of Calgary's most architecturally interesting communities. Hidden pathways get you off the beaten path in the heart of Elbow Park and take you to great mountain views at the edge of Mount Royal. The end of your trek follows the Elbow River through the community of Riverdale. Hill options with lots of saskatoon berries make the end of your outing a tasty treat in the heart of summer.

Seasonal Highlights/ Cautions

Fall: Sandy Beach and River Park are a kaleidoscope of rich autumn colours—burnt orange, terracotta, and vibrant yellows glow against rich blue skies.
Winter: Early-morning hoarfrost often covers trees close to the Elbow River.
Winter and Spring: The treed trail from Sandy Beach to River Park can be slippery in the winter and spring. An alternative is to follow the paved path or road uphill to River Park.

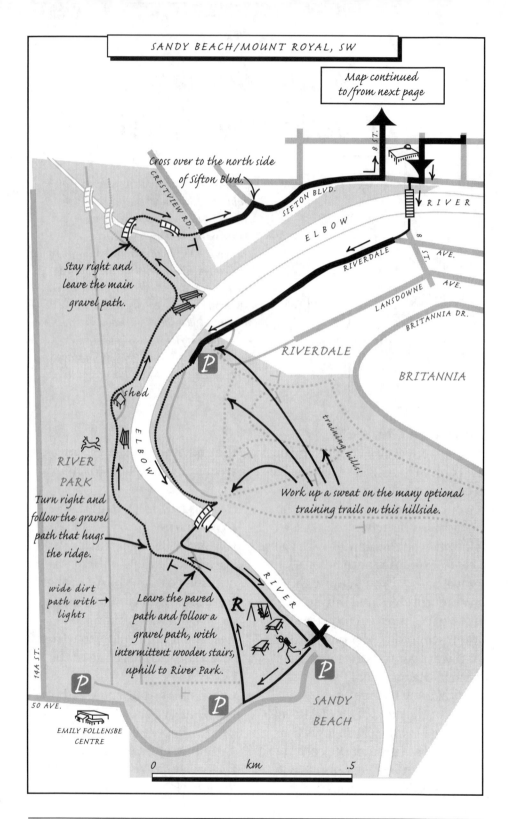

Map continued to/from next page

8 ST.

Cross over to the north side of Sifton Blvd.

CRESTVIEW RD.

SIFTON BLVD.

ELBOW

RIVER

Stay right and leave the main gravel path.

RIVERDALE

8 ST.

AVE.

LANSDOWNE AVE.

BRITANNIA DR.

RIVERDALE

BRITANNIA

shed

ELBOW

RIVER PARK

Turn right and follow the gravel path that hugs the ridge.

training hills!

Work up a sweat on the many optional training trails on this hillside.

wide dirt path with lights

Leave the paved path and follow a gravel path, with intermittent wooden stairs, uphill to River Park.

R

RIVER

14A ST.

50 AVE.

EMILY FOLLENSBE CENTRE

SANDY BEACH

0   km   .5

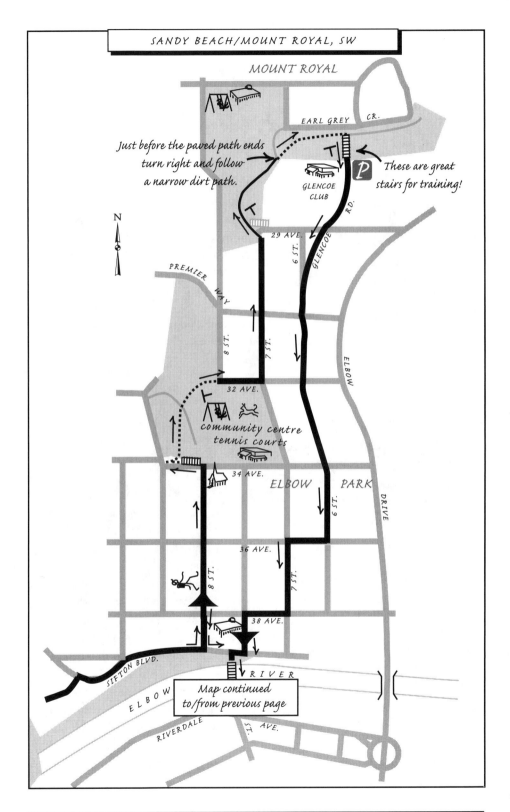

SANDY BEACH/MOUNT ROYAL, SW

MOUNT ROYAL

EARL GREY CR.

Just before the paved path ends
turn right and follow
a narrow dirt path.

These are great
stairs for training!

GLENCOE CLUB

N

29 AVE.

6 ST.

GLENCOE RD.

PREMIER WAY

8 ST.

7 ST.

ELBOW

32 AVE.

community centre
tennis courts

ELBOW   PARK   DRIVE

34 AVE.

6 ST.

36 AVE.

7 ST.

8 ST.

38 AVE.

SIFTON BLVD.

RIVER

Map continued
to/from previous page

ELBOW

RIVERDALE

7 ST. AVE.

Britannia/
Park Hill, SW

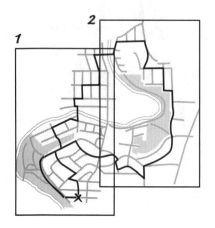

Categories: *neighbourhood*
Approximate Distance: *6 kilometres*
Approximate Time: *1–1.5 hours*
Degree of Difficulty: *easy, with one hill; many hill-training options*
Parking: *at the intersection of 49 Avenue and Elbow Drive, turn into Britannia Plaza; park anywhere along 49 Avenue*
Facilities: *none*

Hike at a Glance

A hike that starts outside a Dutch chocolate and pastry shop is bound to be a good one! From the specialty shopping plaza in Britannia, hike south to views of the Elbow River. It is said that this was a prime buffalo jump location. Bones have been found at the base of the Britannia cliffs, where generations of Natives stampeded buffalo. Today, it is a prime location for hill climbing, so get to it! The remainder of the hike follows sidewalks through quiet neighbourhoods. The homes, gardens, and in winter, the interior design ideas and Christmas light displays make this an uplifting hike throughout the year.

Nature Note

URBAN COYOTES

The bright lights of the big city have not deterred coyotes. I've seen pups playing near the river not far from Sandy Beach. As members of the dog family, they look like dogs. Coyotes are gray on top, brown on the sides, and pale underneath. It's not unusual to hear them yapping or howling when fire engine sirens wail nearby. Coyotes munch on rodents, berries, snowshoe hares, and in the spring, newborn deer. Even though they tend to run from humans, they are very opportunistic and will approach small children and dogs. City coyotes also enjoy cat casserole, so keep Fluffy close by.

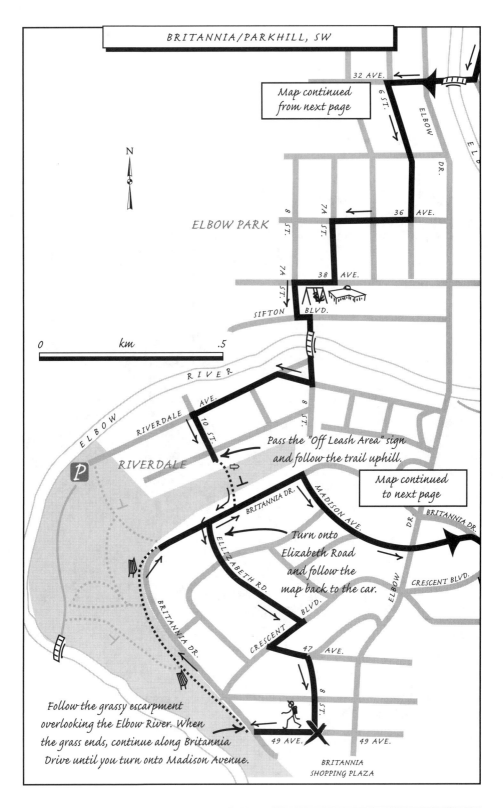

32 AVE.

9 ST.

Map continued from next page

ELBOW DR.

ELBOW

N

ELBOW PARK

8 ST.

74 ST.

36 AVE.

74 ST.

38 AVE.

SIFTON BLVD.

0   km   .5

RIVER

ELBOW

RIVERDALE AVE.

10 ST.

8 ST.

RIVERDALE

Pass the "Off Leash Area" sign and follow the trail uphill.

Map continued to next page

BRITANNIA DR.

MADISON AVE.

ELBOW DR.

BRITANNIA DR.

ELIZABETH RD.

Turn onto Elizabeth Road and follow the map back to the car.

CRESCENT BLVD.

BRITANNIA DR.

CRESCENT BLVD.

47 AVE.

8 ST.

Follow the grassy escarpment overlooking the Elbow River. When the grass ends, continue along Britannia Drive until you turn onto Madison Avenue.

49 AVE.

49 AVE.

BRITANNIA SHOPPING PLAZA

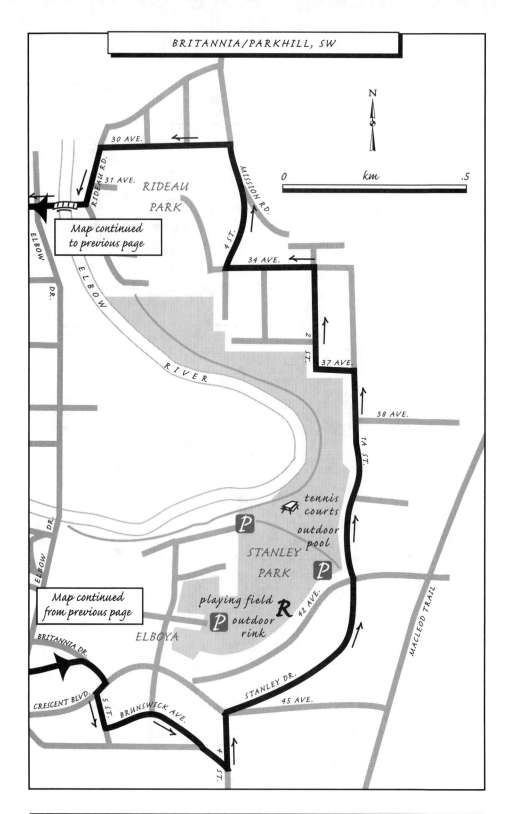

N

0   km   .5

30 AVE.

RIDEAU RD.

31 AVE.

RIDEAU
PARK

MISSION RD.

4 ST.

Map continued
to previous page

ELBOW DR.

ELBOW

RIVER

34 AVE.

2 ST.

37 AVE.

38 AVE.

1A ST.

tennis
courts

outdoor
pool

STANLEY

PARK

ELBOW DR.

Map continued
from previous page

playing field

outdoor
rink

R

42 AVE.

ELBOYA

MACLEOD TRAIL

BRITANNIA DR.

CRESCENT BLVD.

1 ST.

BRUNSWICK AVE.

STANLEY DR.

45 AVE.

4 ST.

Beaverdam Flats/ Carburn Park, SE

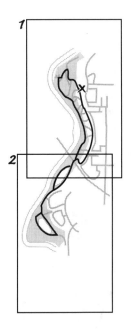

Category: nature
Approximate Distance: 7 kilometres
Approximate Time: 1.25 hours
Degree of Difficulty: easy, with one mandatory hill at the end; lots of hill-climbing options along the escarpment
Parking: official parking lot at the intersection of Lynnview Way and Lynnview Road
Facilities: bathrooms (open from May to September); picnic tables; barbecue pits

Hike at a Glance

Descend into the river valley to Beaverdam Flats Park. This flat route follows the river on paved, shale, and dirt paths through poplar forest, shrubs, and grassland. Beaverdam Flats and Carburn Park have been reclaimed from former industrial sites and now make up a single natural environment park. When the trees are fully leafed out, this extensive green space becomes a hidden oasis of rivers, lakes, and plentiful bird life. In fact, you may see American white pelicans, double-crested cormorants, and bald eagles on this route. Even though you could hike all the way to Fish Creek Park from here, this route loops around the lake at Carburn Park, back up to Beaverdam Flats.

Seasonal Highlights/ Cautions

Fall: An abundance of trees makes this a colourful fall trek.
Winter: When the trees are bare, this route can be noisy from traffic on Glenmore Trail.

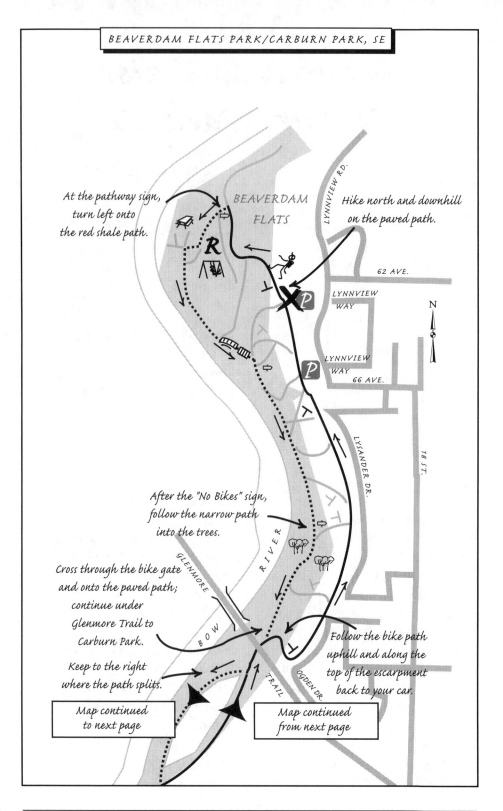

At the pathway sign, turn left onto the red shale path.

BEAVERDAM FLATS

Hike north and downhill on the paved path.

LYNNVIEW RD.

62 AVE.

LYNNVIEW WAY

N

LYNNVIEW WAY
66 AVE.

LYSANDER DR.

18 ST.

After the "No Bikes" sign, follow the narrow path into the trees.

GLENMORE

RIVER

Cross through the bike gate and onto the paved path; continue under Glenmore Trail to Carburn Park.

BOW

Keep to the right where the path splits.

TRAIL

OGDEN DR.

Follow the bike path uphill and along the top of the escarpment back to your car.

Map continued to next page

Map continued from next page

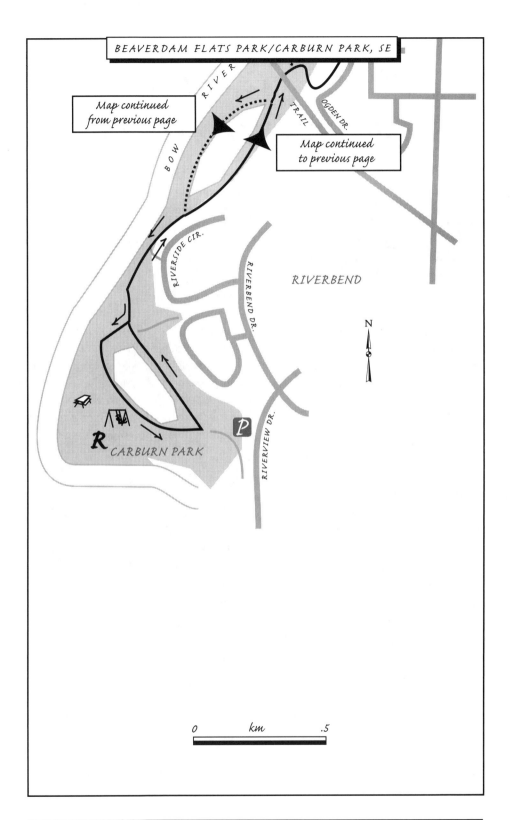

Map continued
from previous page

Map continued
to previous page

BOW RIVER

OGDEN DR.

TRAIL

RIVERSIDE CIR.

RIVERBEND DR.

RIVERBEND

N

RIVERVIEW DR.

R CARBURN PARK

0   km   .5

Weaselhead Flats/ North Glenmore Park, SW

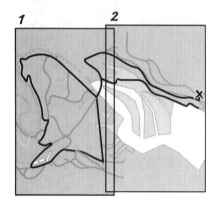

Categories: *nature, kids, coffee shop*
Approximate Distance: *8 kilometres*
Approximate Time: *2 hours*
Degree of Difficulty: *from both parking lot "E" or the Weaselhead parking lot, the route is easy, mostly flat with one mandatory hill and some optional hills*
Parking: *There are two starting points. If you want a shorter hike, start at the Weaselhead parking area, marked with a sign. For a longer hike, start at parking lot "E" in North Glenmore Park with access from 37 Street or Crowchild Trail.*
Facilities: *bathrooms at parking lot "E" and Weaselhead parking lot (outhouse open year round); bathrooms (open from May to September); picnic tables; barbecues; playgrounds*

Hike at a Glance

If you want solitude, then this is the hike for you. A relatively flat hike that starts in North Glenmore Park follows well-used dirt trails along the shore of the reservoir. A paved-path route along the top of the escarpment is an option when the water is high and covers the lower trails. This is the most peaceful hike in the city, with the sounds of birds chirping, and ducks landing and flapping overhead. The untrained eye will spot bald eagles, all kinds of ducks, geese and goslings (in the spring), and red-winged blackbirds. The hiker sporting binoculars with bird book in hand will be very busy keeping watch for up to seventy bird species that frequent the park. A short stint on the paved path leads to the shady Weaselhead trails. Interpretive signs mark the route that twists and turns along the Elbow River. Deer, coyotes, rabbits, and the occasional black bear and moose are your hidden hiking companions. Listen for the pileated woodpecker that rocks his noggin making huge holes in dead trees. This is true wilderness.

Nature Note

NATURAL AREAS

Weaselhead Flats is a natural area. Natural areas are pieces of land left in a natural state. Calgary's natural environment parks often contain unique or unusual vegetation, such as the 400-year-old Douglas fir trees on the Douglas Fir Trail; historical components, such as the teepee rings at Nose Hill Park; or animals, like the large moose that rely on the Edgemont Ravine for a travel corridor.

PRIMAL GROUNDS CAFÉ

Primal Grounds Café has great home-made organic food described by the slogan "The way Mom used to make it." I love the cakes and will drive out of my way when a cake craving hits. Do an extra hill or two if you have a sweet tooth! Location: 3003-37 Street SW

Weaselhead Flats Natural Area is year-round nature hiking at its best.

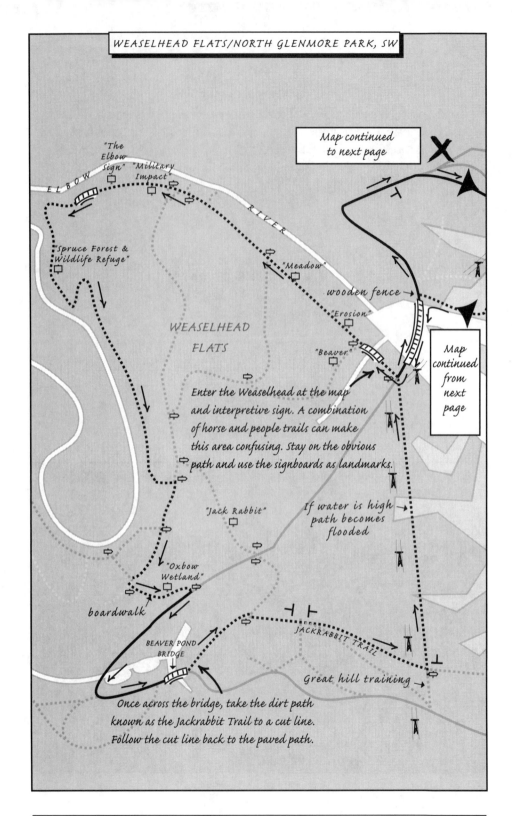

Map continued
to next page

"The
Elbow
Sign"   "Military
Impact"

E L B O W

R I V E R

"Spruce Forest &
Wildlife Refuge"

"Meadow"

wooden fence →

"Erosion"

WEASELHEAD
FLATS

"Beaver"

Map
continued
from
next
page

Enter the Weaselhead at the map
and interpretive sign. A combination
of horse and people trails can make
this area confusing. Stay on the obvious
path and use the signboards as landmarks.

"Jack Rabbit"

If water is high
path becomes
flooded

"Oxbow
Wetland"

boardwalk

BEAVER POND
BRIDGE

JACKRABBIT TRAIL

Great hill training →

Once across the bridge, take the dirt path
known as the Jackrabbit Trail to a cut line.
Follow the cut line back to the paved path.

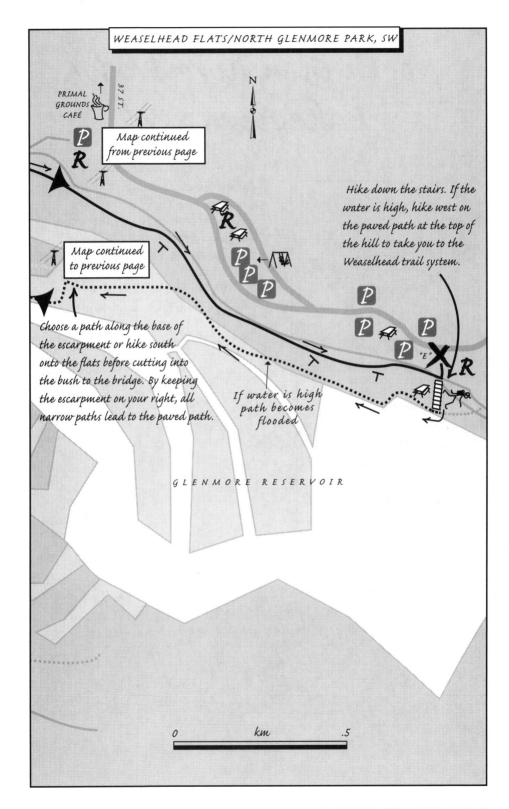

N

PRIMAL GROUNDS CAFÉ

37 ST.

Map continued from previous page

Hike down the stairs. If the water is high, hike west on the paved path at the top of the hill to take you to the Weaselhead trail system.

Map continued to previous page

Choose a path along the base of the escarpment or hike south onto the flats before cutting into the bush to the bridge. By keeping the escarpment on your right, all narrow paths lead to the paved path.

If water is high path becomes flooded

"E"

GLENMORE RESERVOIR

0   km   .5

North Glenmore Park/ Lakeview, SW

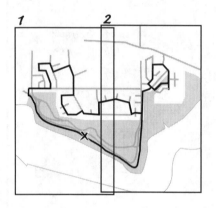

Category: park/neighbourhood

Approximate Distance: 7 kilometres

Approximate Time: 1.5 hours

Degree of Difficulty: easy and flat

Parking: official parking lot "E" in North Glenmore Park, accessed from 37 Street or Crowchild Trail

Facilities: bathroom (outhouse open year round); picnic tables; barbecues; playgrounds

Hike at a Glance

This flat route makes for a pleasant after-dinner stroll. The paved path follows the escarpment edge overlooking the Glenmore Reservoir. Watch for coyotes running across the ice in the winter. Pass the Calgary Canoe Club and enter the community of Lakeview. Enjoy a neighbourhood stroll past beautiful homes with well-kept yards and mature trees.

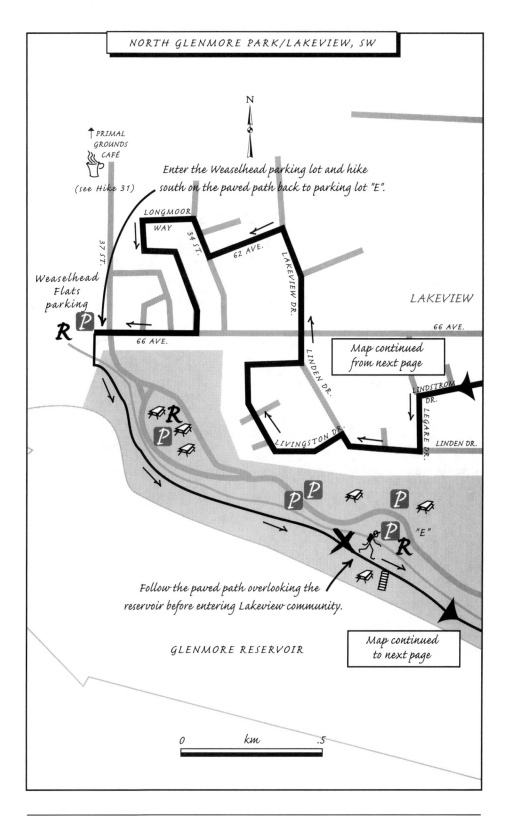

↑ PRIMAL
GROUNDS
CAFÉ

(see Hike 31)

Enter the Weaselhead parking lot and hike
south on the paved path back to parking lot "E".

N

LONGMOOR
WAY

37 ST.

34 ST.

62 AVE.

LAKEVIEW DR.

Weaselhead
Flats
parking

R P

66 AVE.

66 AVE.

LAKEVIEW

66 AVE.

Map continued
from next page

LINDEN DR.

LINDSTROM DR.

LEGARE DR.

LINDEN DR.

R P

LIVINGSTON DR.

P P

P

P R "E"

X

Follow the paved path overlooking the
reservoir before entering Lakeview community.

GLENMORE RESERVOIR

Map continued
to next page

0   km   .5

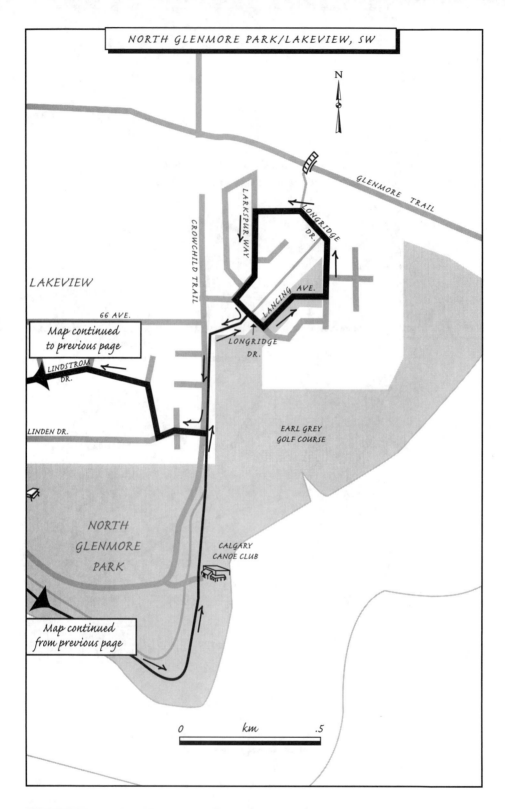

N

GLENMORE TRAIL

LARKSPUR WAY

CROWCHILD TRAIL

LONGRIDGE DR.

LANCING AVE.

LAKEVIEW

66 AVE.

Map continued
to previous page

LINDSTROM
DR.

LONGRIDGE
DR.

LINDEN DR.

EARL GREY
GOLF COURSE

NORTH
GLENMORE
PARK

CALGARY
CANOE CLUB

Map continued
from previous page

0   km   .5

Jackrabbit Trail, SW

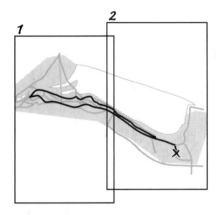

Categories: *nature, kids, coffee shop, trail training*

Approximate Distance: *7 kilometres*

Approximate Time: *1.5 hours*

Degree of Difficulty: *moderate, with rolling hills on the way out; easy, flat paved path on the return*

Parking: *At the intersection of 90 Avenue and 24 Street, turn north on 24 Street towards the reservoir; take the first left and park in the official parking lot*

Facilities: *bathroom at sailing school (open from May to September); playground*

Hike at a Glance

Kids love this single-track trek through the forest. Rolling dirt paths turn to gravel, offering reservoir views that are a welcome sight for homesick east- or west-coasters who crave large bodies of water. If you stop and listen, you will hear the chirp of chickadees, who are well fed and will land on your hand in search of seeds. The loop back follows a popular paved path covered by a canopy of trees. This is another gem of a hike in the heart of Calgary!

Seasonal Highlights/ Cautions

Fall: A trail highlight is the leafy canopy of rich fall colours.

Winter and Spring: Snow-covered trails can be slippery after a Chinook and during the spring thaw.

GOOD EARTH CAFÉ

The Good Earth Café offers fresh-roasted coffee and a full menu of baked goods, lunches, and desserts. I'm like a chickadee and go for their toasted seed buns that are covered with sunflower, sesame, and pumpkin seeds. Take one of their sandwiches on your trek. They are tasty and tough, so they will not be squashed in your backpack. Location: Glenmore Landing, 90 Avenue and 14 Street SW.

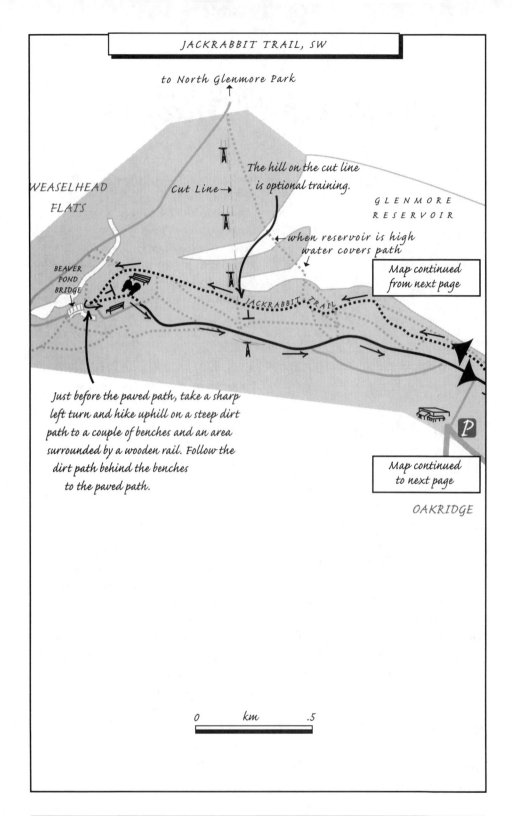

to North Glenmore Park

WEASELHEAD
FLATS

Cut Line →

The hill on the cut line
is optional training.

GLENMORE
RESERVOIR

← when reservoir is high
water covers path

BEAVER
POND
BRIDGE

JACKRABBIT TRAIL

Map continued
from next page

Map continued
to next page

OAKRIDGE

Just before the paved path, take a sharp
left turn and hike uphill on a steep dirt
path to a couple of benches and an area
surrounded by a wooden rail. Follow the
dirt path behind the benches
to the paved path.

0   km   .5

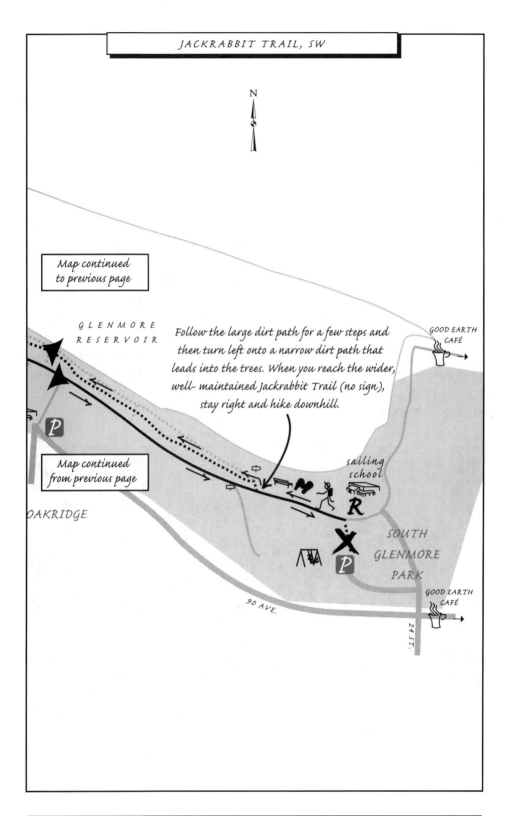

N

Map continued
to previous page

GLENMORE
RESERVOIR

Follow the large dirt path for a few steps and
then turn left onto a narrow dirt path that
leads into the trees. When you reach the wider,
well- maintained Jackrabbit Trail (no sign),
stay right and hike downhill.

GOOD EARTH
CAFÉ

Map continued
from previous page

OAKRIDGE

sailing
school

R

SOUTH
GLENMORE
PARK

90 AVE.

24 ST.

GOOD EARTH
CAFÉ

Fish Creek Provincial Park: An Overview

Fish Creek Provincial Park is perfect for people who tend to get bored easily. It is large and full of trails, wildlife, flora and fauna, and a tempting café and restaurant. So before heading out, you should choose your hiking angle. Bring your hiking poles and backpack and do some hill training. Bring a picnic lunch and enjoy a leisurely family outing with your dog, kids, or baby in backpack. Binocular-clad hikers can get up close and personal with the wildlife. Photographers can immortalize the wildlife, wildflowers, or the many shades of autumn. In a year with good snow, the cross-country skiing is a treat in the heart of the city. The routes described here mostly follow red shale paths over bridges, with some paved and dirt-path sections. They offer a good overview of the 1,150 hectares of park and close to 80 kilometres of trails available for exploration. Each season has its highlights, so take to the pathways and see something new!

A sunny summer hike near Bow Valley Ranch in Fish Creek Park is the perfect urban nature escape.

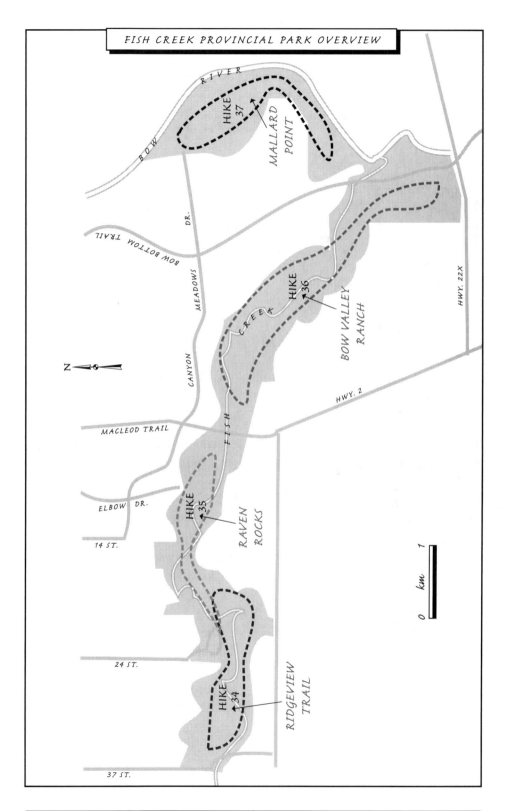

FISH CREEK PROVINCIAL PARK OVERVIEW

Ridgeview Trail (Fish Creek), SW

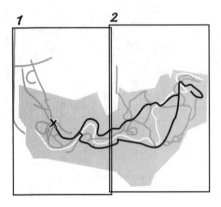

Categories: nature, trail training, kids
Approximate Distance: 7 kilometres
Approximate Time: 1.5 hours
Degree of Difficulty: moderate, with rolling hills; many training options
Parking: from 130 Avenue, turn south onto Wood Path Road; keep left at the Y-intersection and continue to the first parking lot
Facilities: bathrooms (open year round); picnic tables; barbecue pits

Hike at a Glance

Towering white spruce forests offer a shaded canopy on the Ridgeview Trail hike. This rolling trail is a combination of narrow dirt paths with occasional stairs, narrow training hills, wide shale pathways, and a short stretch on paved paths. From woodland to wetland, you hike through a variety of habitats. The plant life you will see includes wild roses, red raspberries, abundant saskatoons, violets, asters, and goldenrods. Wildlife viewing gives you many opportunities to stop.

Watch for the mule deer between bridges #4 and #6, and listen for the pileated woodpecker who lives off the ants and beetles in the old-growth forest at the beginning of the trek. Keep a keen eye open for the woodpecker's trademark, a large rectangular hole in tree trunks.

Seasonal Highlights/ Cautions

Winter and Spring: It can be very icy underfoot in late winter and early spring.

Nature Notes

DEER DIFFERENCES

Impress your friends with some nature knowledge.

Mule deer: They have large ears rimmed with black and tails that are white with a black tip. Mule deer travel in small bands of does, yearlings, and fawns; the bucks travel alone.

White-tails: They have brown tails, but when alarmed, they lift their tails to expose the white underside and a white rump patch, waving their furry flag to warn their friends. Being quite solitary and shy, white-tails usually travel alone or with the current year's offspring.

RAVEN OR CROW?

Since ravens are mountain and northern forest birds, it is unique to have them nesting in the parkland and prairies. Cliffs are their favourite nesting spot, which is where they can be found in Fish Creek. Usually larger and with a heavier bill than crows, ravens soar overhead, while crows flap their wings steadily. Smart scavengers, ravens will eat anything. They talk to each other with "rawks" and "tocks," but it is the gutteral "croak" made by the raven that gives it away.

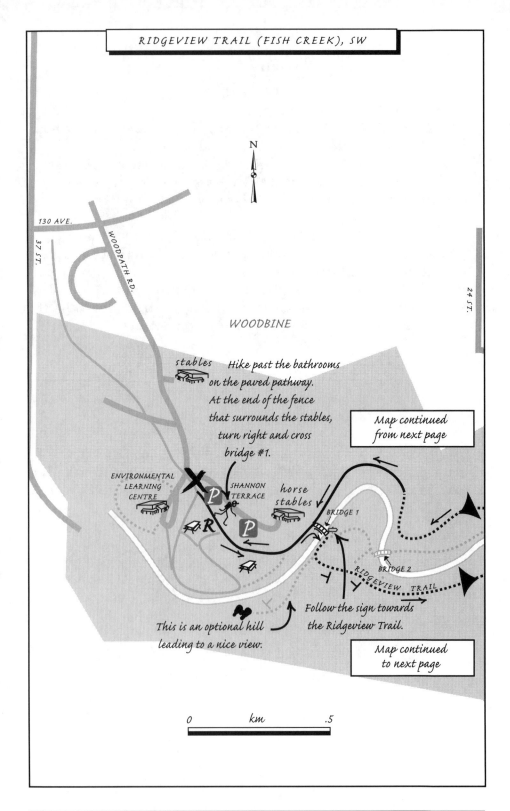

N

130 AVE.

37 ST.

WOODPATH RD.

24 ST.

WOODBINE

stables

Hike past the bathrooms on the paved pathway. At the end of the fence that surrounds the stables, turn right and cross bridge #1.

Map continued from next page

ENVIRONMENTAL LEARNING CENTRE

P

SHANNON TERRACE

horse stables

BRIDGE 1

R

P

BRIDGE 2

RIDGEVIEW TRAIL

Follow the sign towards the Ridgeview Trail.

This is an optional hill leading to a nice view.

Map continued to next page

0   km   .5

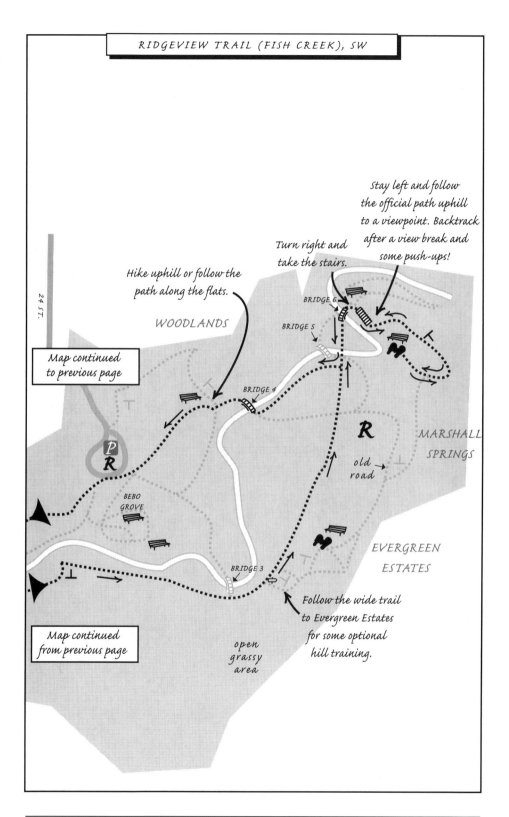

24 ST.

Stay left and follow
the official path uphill
to a viewpoint. Backtrack
after a view break and
some push-ups!

Turn right and
take the stairs.

Hike uphill or follow the
path along the flats.

BRIDGE 6

WOODLANDS

BRIDGE 5

Map continued
to previous page

BRIDGE 4

MARSHALL
SPRINGS

R

old
road

BEBO
GROVE

EVERGREEN
ESTATES

BRIDGE 3

Map continued
from previous page

Follow the wide trail
to Evergreen Estates
for some optional
hill training.

open
grassy
area

Raven Rocks (Fish Creek), SW

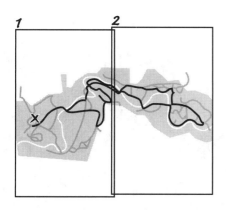

Categories: nature, kids
Approximate Distance: 7 kilometres
Approximate Time: 1.75 hours
Degree of Difficulty: easy, mainly flat; trail training options make it more challenging
Parking: follow 24 Street south into Bebo Grove parking lot
Facilities: bathroom (open year round); picnic tables; barbecue pits

Hike at a Glance

From the wide open grasslands around the Bebo Grove parking lot, you make your way into spruce and aspen forests that offer shade and great wildlife-viewing opportunities. I always see mule deer while hiking in this area and if you look up—way up—you may see a great horned owl sitting in the poplar trees. Downstream from Bebo Grove, hike past sandstone cliffs on the north side of the creek. Once quarried for use in con- struction in the early 1900s, the sandstone was eventually found to be too soft and its use was discontinued. The cliffs are favourite nesting spots for ravens, so keep your ears and eyes peeled for soaring sights and guttural squawks.

Seasonal Highlights/ Cautions

Winter: The trails can be slip- pery in winter.

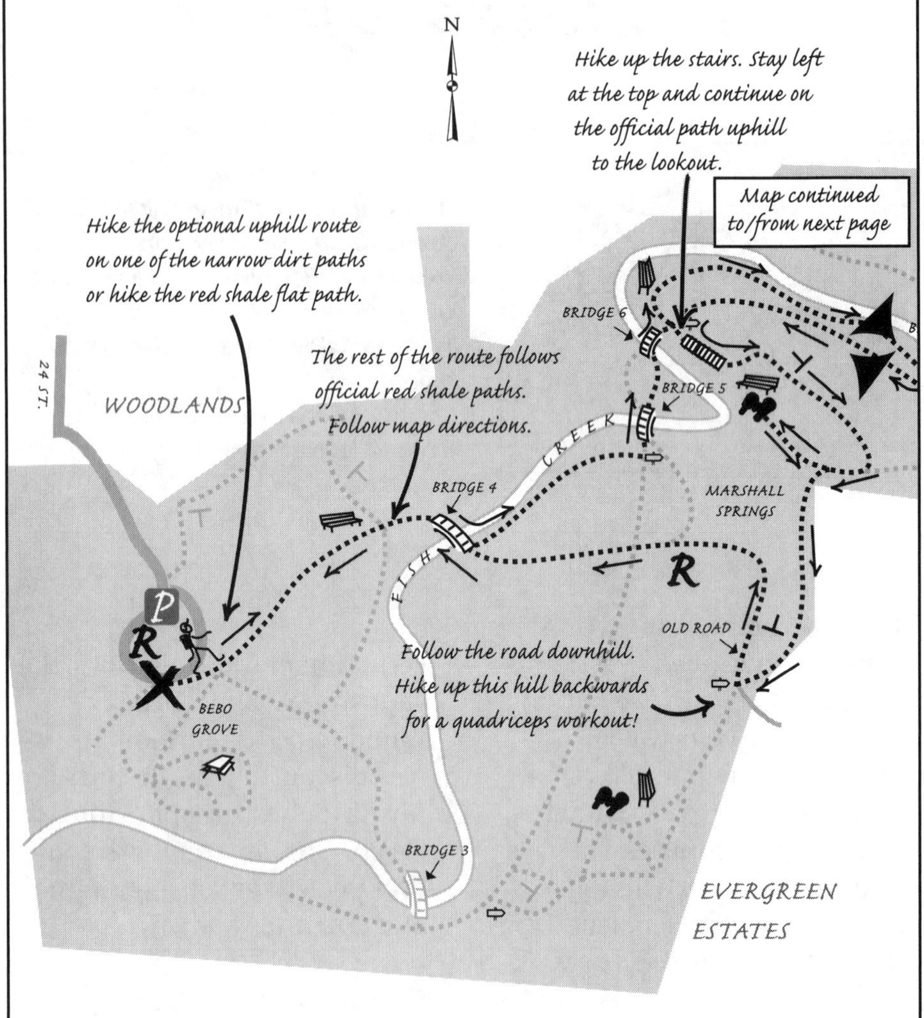

N

Hike up the stairs. Stay left
at the top and continue on
the official path uphill
to the lookout.

Map continued
to/from next page

Hike the optional uphill route
on one of the narrow dirt paths
or hike the red shale flat path.

BRIDGE 6

24 ST.

WOODLANDS

The rest of the route follows
official red shale paths.
Follow map directions.

BRIDGE 5

CREEK

BRIDGE 4

MARSHALL
SPRINGS

FISH

R

P

R

X

OLD ROAD

BEBO
GROVE

Follow the road downhill.
Hike up this hill backwards
for a quadriceps workout!

BRIDGE 3

EVERGREEN
ESTATES

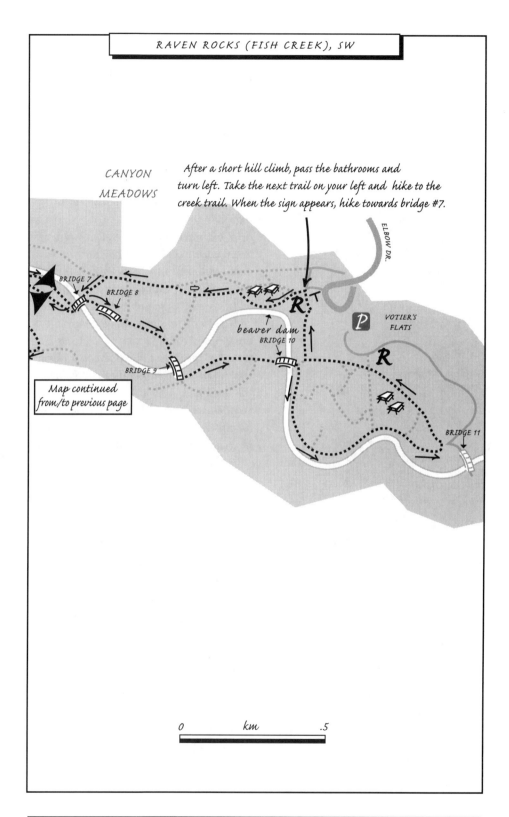

CANYON
MEADOWS

After a short hill climb, pass the bathrooms and
turn left. Take the next trail on your left and hike to the
creek trail. When the sign appears, hike towards bridge #7.

ELBOW DR.

BRIDGE 7

BRIDGE 8

R

VOTIER'S
FLATS

beaver dam
BRIDGE 10

R

BRIDGE 9

Map continued
from/to previous page

BRIDGE 11

0   km   .5

Bow Valley Ranch (Fish Creek), SE

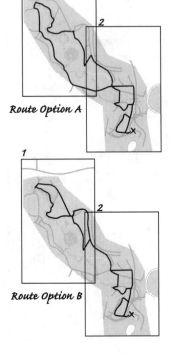

Route Option A

Route Option B

Categories: *nature, trail training, coffee shop, kids*

Approximate Distance: *8 kilometres*

Approximate Time: *2.75 hours (for a shorter hike, start from Bow Valley Ranch)*

Degree of Difficulty: *moderate, with a mix of flats and hills; use Map A for the flat route, and use Map B for some hill training.*

Parking: *take Bow Bottom Trail into Fish Creek Park; just past the Hull's Wood parking lot, turn right and park at the first Sikome Lake parking lot*

Facilities: *bathroom (open year round); visitor centre; phone booth; picnic tables; restaurant; café (open from May to September)*

Hike at a Glance

Wide-open native grasslands with a scattering of trees make up the eastern end of the park. A combination of mountain viewpoints, steep-slope climbs, and wandering creek trails, it is the perfect year-round loop. The return portion of the hike lets you choose between two routes, a hilly one or a mostly flat one. Wildlife sightings are common in this area. In the morning and evenings, mule deer graze on shrubs near the parking lot and long-necked, long-legged great blue herons feed in the creek near the bridge. Stop at the information centre to learn more about the natural and cultural history of the area and then treat yourself to a tasty treat at Annie's Café or a decadent dinner at the Ranche Restaurant.

Seasonal Highlights/ Cautions

Spring and Summer: Great blue herons can be seen along the creek.

Nature Note

WORKAHOLIC BEAVERS

Just past the ranch area, you will start to see beaver dams in the streams and many fallen trees along the stream banks. Beavers use the trees to build dams; they also eat the bark, leaves, and twigs. Beavers are a bit driven. For instance, they are attracted to the sound of water running over a dam. Place a radio with the sound of running water close to a beaver and watch the building frenzy that erupts while she buries the radio until the sound is muted. Do beavers ever stop building? Perhaps in the short term, like during winter, but not in the long term. Eventually their food runs out and then they dismantle the dam, move on, and start from scratch somewhere else.

Annie's Bakery and Café is open on the weekends during the winter months.

ANNIE'S BAKERY AND CAFÉ

Once part of the Patrick Burns ranching and meat-packing empire, Fish Creek was purchased by the provincial government in 1973. In 1997 restoration of the ranch buildings began and Annie's Café was born. Originally the foreman's house, this cozy café is named after Annie Bannister, the foreman's wife. The ranch feeling is alive at Annie's where the kitchen uses an antique stove to heat homemade soups, and the rooms are filled with rickety wooden chairs and artifacts from the ranching past. Muffins, scones, and cookies tempt post-hike taste buds. From Victoria Day in May until Labour Day in September, Annie's is open daily. For the rest of the year, it is only open on weekends. Location: Fish Creek Park, Bow Valley Ranch; Phone: 225-3920

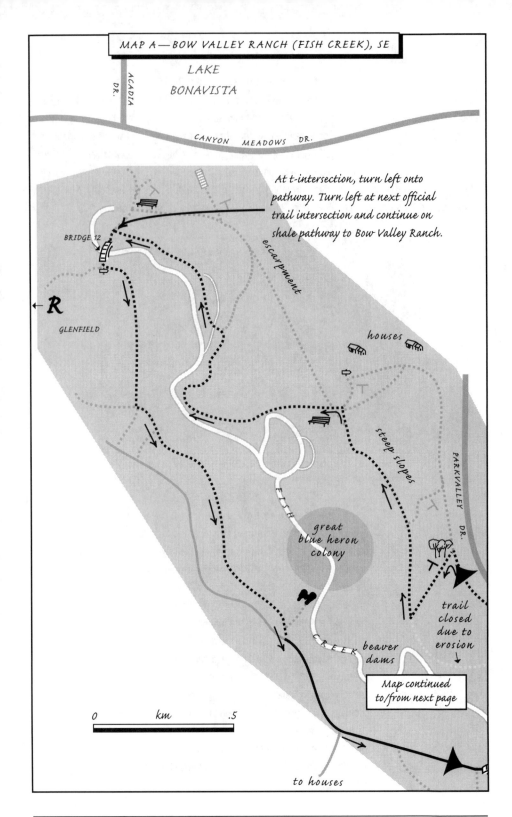

LAKE
BONAVISTA

ACADIA DR.

CANYON MEADOWS DR.

At t-intersection, turn left onto
pathway. Turn left at next official
trail intersection and continue on
shale pathway to Bow Valley Ranch.

escarpment

BRIDGE 12

R

GLENFIELD

houses

steep slopes

PARKVALLEY DR.

FISH

great
blue heron
colony

trail
closed
due to
erosion

CREEK

beaver
dams

Map continued
to/from next page

0   km   .5

to houses

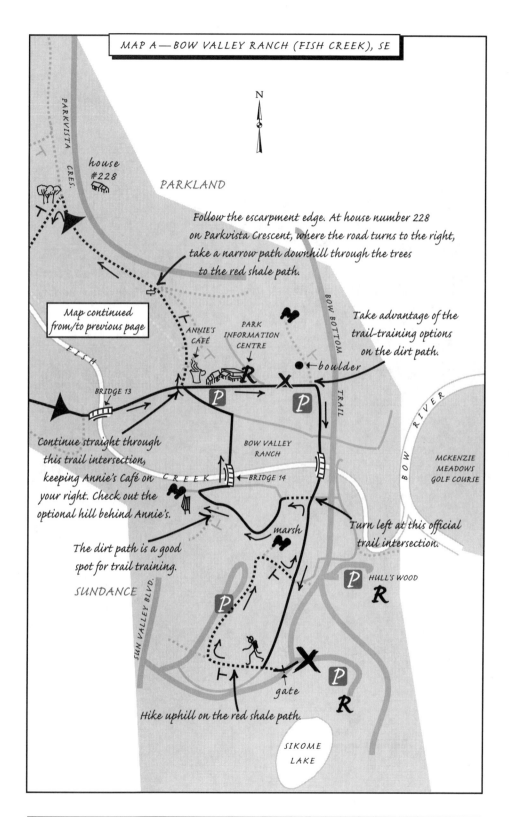

N

PARKVISTA CRES.

house #228

PARKLAND

Follow the escarpment edge. At house number 228 on Parkvista Crescent, where the road turns to the right, take a narrow path downhill through the trees to the red shale path.

Map continued from/to previous page

FISH

ANNIE'S CAFÉ

PARK INFORMATION CENTRE

BOW BOTTOM TRAIL

Take advantage of the trail-training options on the dirt path.

←boulder

BRIDGE 13

P

P

BOW RIVER

Continue straight through this trail intersection, keeping Annie's Café on your right. Check out the optional hill behind Annie's.

CREEK

BOW VALLEY RANCH

←BRIDGE 14

MCKENZIE MEADOWS GOLF COURSE

The dirt path is a good spot for trail training.

SUNDANCE

marsh

Turn left at this official trail intersection.

SUN VALLEY BLVD.

P

P

HULL'S WOOD

R

Hike uphill on the red shale path.

gate

P

R

SIKOME LAKE

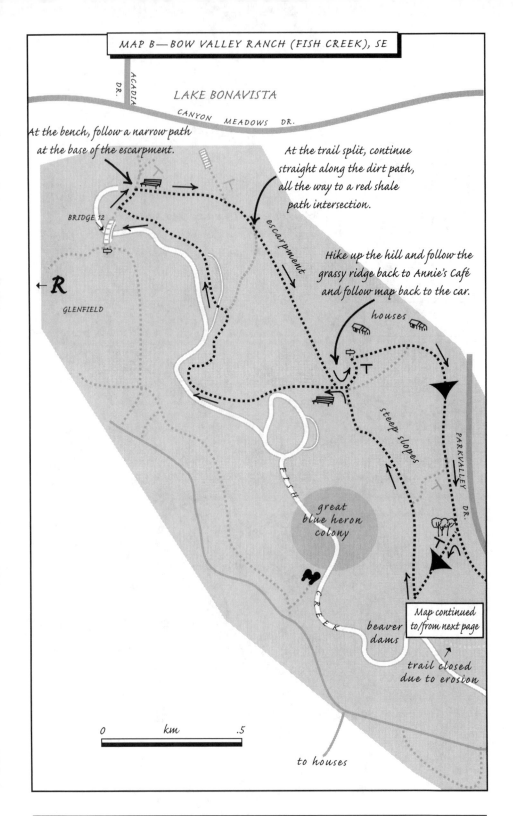

LAKE BONAVISTA

ACADIA DR.

CANYON MEADOWS DR.

At the bench, follow a narrow path at the base of the escarpment.

At the trail split, continue straight along the dirt path, all the way to a red shale path intersection.

BRIDGE 12

escarpment

Hike up the hill and follow the grassy ridge back to Annie's Café and follow map back to the car.

R

GLENFIELD

houses

FISH

great blue heron colony

steep slopes

PARKVALLEY DR.

Map continued to/from next page

CREEK

beaver dams

trail closed due to erosion

0   km   .5

to houses

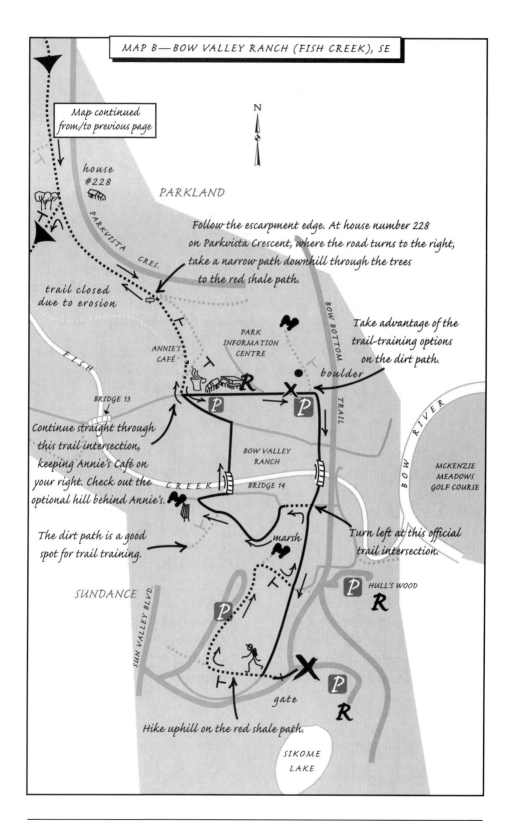

N

Map continued
from/to previous page

house
#228

PARKLAND

PARKVISTA CRES.

Follow the escarpment edge. At house number 228
on Parkvista Crescent, where the road turns to the right,
take a narrow path downhill through the trees
to the red shale path.

trail closed
due to erosion

FISH

ANNIE'S
CAFÉ

PARK
INFORMATION
CENTRE

BOW BOTTOM

boulder

Take advantage of the
trail-training options
on the dirt path.

TRAIL

R

P

P

BRIDGE 13

BOW VALLEY
RANCH

BOW RIVER

MCKENZIE
MEADOWS
GOLF COURSE

Continue straight through
this trail intersection,
keeping Annie's Café on
your right. Check out the
optional hill behind Annie's.

CREEK

BRIDGE 14

The dirt path is a good
spot for trail training.

marsh

Turn left at this official
trail intersection.

SUNDANCE

SUN VALLEY BLVD.

P

HULL'S WOOD

R

P

gate

P

R

Hike uphill on the red shale path.

SIKOME
LAKE

Mallard Point (Fish Creek), SE

Category: nature, kids
Approximate Distance: 7 kilometres
Approximate Time: 1.5 hours
Degree of Difficulty: easy and flat
Parking: official Fish Creek parking lot at the end of Canyon Meadows Drive
Facilities: bathrooms (open year round); picnic tables

Hike at a Glance

Located at the easternmost end of the park, Mallard Point is a duck hangout. Year round, birds of prey sit high in treetops, while beavers fight off the geese and the ducks socialize. A favourite spot for bird watching, it is a hive of activity in the spring when the birds are bickering over nesting spots. Poplars, water birch, willows, and cow parsnip line the route that meanders along the creek and makes a perfect post-dinner stroll. Watch for woodpeckers, nuthatches, tree swallows, wrens, and a variety of water birds. If you need some peace and quiet, head out to Mallard Point after a fresh snowfall, in the early morning on a blue-sky day.

Seasonal Highlights/ Cautions

Winter: After a fresh snowfall, this is the perfect spot for a peaceful stroll.

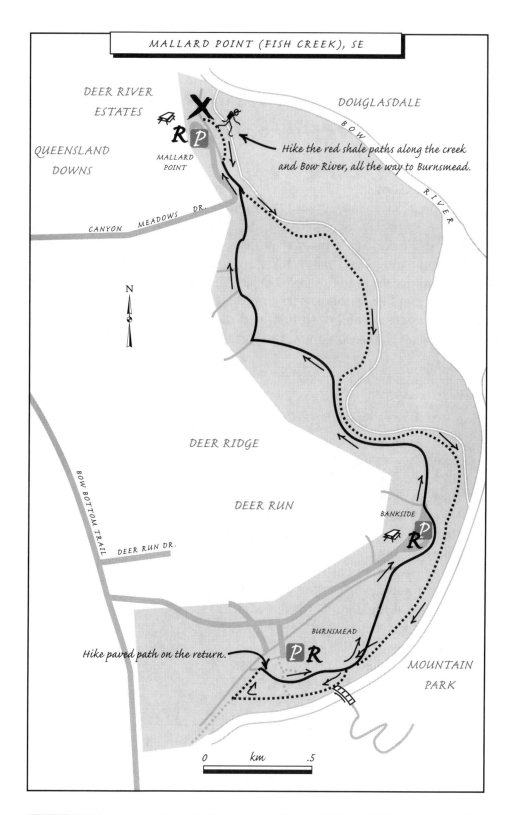

DEER RIVER ESTATES

QUEENSLAND DOWNS

DOUGLASDALE

BOW RIVER

MALLARD POINT

Hike the red shale paths along the creek and Bow River, all the way to Burnsmead.

CANYON MEADOWS DR.

N

DEER RIDGE

DEER RUN

BOW BOTTOM TRAIL

DEER RUN DR.

BANKSIDE

BURNSMEAD

Hike paved path on the return.

MOUNTAIN PARK

0   km   .5

APPENDIX

The Best of Calgary's Best Hikes and Walks

Introduction

This appendix has categorized the guidebook hikes to suit a variety of interests. *Rainy day hikes* get you out of the house even when it's a bit soggy outside and *winter wonderland hikes* are a refreshing start on a crisp January morning. *Trail training* hikes are full of hills so you can work up a sweat and *easy hikes* follow mostly flat terrain through Calgary's most beautiful neighbourhoods, parks, and natural areas. Read through the lists of categories below to help you decide the best places to hike, depending on the season and your interest.

Categories

Trail-Training Hikes (many hills or hill options)

Hike 1: Twelve Mile Coulee, NW
Hike 2: Edgemont Park Ravine, NW
Hike 3: Edgemont Hills, NW
Hike 5: Porcupine Valley (Nose Hill), NW
Hike 6: Rubbing Stone Hill (Nose Hill), NW
Hike 7: Many Owls Valley (Nose Hill), NW
Hike 8: Bowmont Park West, NW
Hike 9: Bowmont Park East, NW
Hike 10: Bowness Park/Bow River, NW
Hike 14: McHugh Bluff/Prince's Island, NW
Hike 16: Bridgeland/Bow River, NE
Hike 18: Edworthy Park, SW
Hike 19: Douglas Fir Trail, SW
Hike 21: Elbow Park/Mount Royal, SW
Hike 24: Roxboro/Stanley Park, SW
Hike 28: Sandy Beach/Mount Royal, SW
Hike 33: Jackrabbit Trail, SW
Hike 34: Ridgeview Trail (Fish Creek), SW
Hike 36b: Bow Valley Ranch (Fish Creek), SE

Easy Hikes (mostly flat with hill options)

Hike 4: West Nose Creek Park, NE
Hike 7: Many Owls Valley (Nose Hill), NW
Hike 10: Bowness Park/Bow River, NW
Hike 11: Bowness/Shouldice Park, NW
Hike 12: Confederation Park/Nose Hill, NW
Hike 13: Briar Hill/Parkdale, NW
Hike 15: Regal Terrace/Sunnyside, NE/NW
Hike 16: Bridgeland/Bow River, NE
Hike 17: Strachcona Ravine, SW
Hike 20: Bow River/Scarboro, SW
Hike 21: Elbow Park/Mount Royal, SW
Hike 23: Inglewood Bird Sanctuary, SE
Hike 26: Garrison Woods/Marda Loop, SW
Hike 27: Glenmore Dam/Bel-Aire, SW
Hike 29: Britannia/Parkhill, SW
Hike 30: Beaverdam Flats Park/Carburn Park, SE
Hike 31: Weaselhead Flats/North Glenmore Park, SW
Hike 32: North Glenmore Park/Lakeview, SW
Hike 35: Raven Rocks (Fish Creek), SW
Hike 36a: Bow Valley Ranch (Fish Creek), SE
Hike 37: Mallard Point (Fish Creek), SE

Rainy Day Hikes

Hike 19: Douglas Fir Trail, SW
Hike 28: Sandy Beach/Mount Royal, SW
Hike 31: Weaselhead Flats/North Glenmore Park, SW
Hike 33: Jackrabbit Trail, SW
Hike 34: Ridgeview Trail (Fish Creek), SW

Kid-Friendly Hikes

Hike 1: Twelve Mile Coulee, NW
Hike 8: Bowmont Park West, NW
Hike 10: Bowness Park/Bow River (short option), NW
Hike 19: Douglas Fir Trail, SW
Hike 31: Weaselhead Flats/North Glenmore Park, SW
Hike 33: Jackrabbit Trail, SW
Hike 34: Ridgeview Trail (Fish Creek), SW
Hike 35: Raven Rocks (Fish Creek), SW
Hike 36: Bow Valley Ranch (Fish Creek), SE
Hike 37: Mallard Point (Fish Creek), SE

Coffee Shop Hikes

Hike 14: McHugh Bluff/Prince's Island, NW
Hike 15: Regal Terrace/Sunnyside, NE/NW
Hike 17: Strathcona Ravine, SW
Hike 18: Edworthy Park, SW
Hike 19: Douglas Fir Trail, SW
Hike 25: Reader Rock Garden/Elbow River, SW
Hike 26: Garrison Woods/Marda Loop, SW
Hike 28: Sandy Beach/Mount Royal, SW
Hike 31: Weaselhead Flats/North Glenmore Park, SW
Hike 33: Jackrabbit Trail, SW
Hike 36: Bow Valley Ranch (Fish Creek), SE

Neighbourhood and Park/Neighbourhood Hikes

Hike 2: Edgemont Park Ravine, NW
Hike 3: Edgemont Hills, NW
Hike 11: Bowness/Shouldice Park, NW
Hike 12: Confederations Park/Nose Hill, NW
Hike 13: Briar Hill/Parkdale, NW
Hike 14: McHugh Bluff/Prince's Island, NW
Hike 15: Regal Terrace/Sunnyside, NE/NW
Hike 16: Bridgeland/Bow River, NE
Hike 17: Strathcona Ravine, SW
Hike 21: Elbow Park/Mount Royal, SW
Hike 22: Ramsay/Inglewood, SE
Hike 24: Roxboro/Stanley Park, SW
Hike 25: Reader Rock Garden/Elbow River, SW
Hike 26: Garrison Woods/Marda Loop, SW
Hike 27: Glenmore Dam/Bel-Aire, SW
Hike 28: Sandy Beach/Mount Royal, SW
Hike 29: Britannia/Parkhill, SW
Hike 32: North Glenmore Park/Lakeview, SW

Nature Hikes (for birds, flowers, and wildlife)

Hike 1: Twelve Mile Coulee, NW
Hike 2: Edgemont Park Ravine, NW
Hike 4: West Nose Creek Park, NE
Hike 5: Porcupine Valley (Nose Hill), NW
Hike 6: Rubbing Stone Hill (Nose Hill), NW
Hike 7: Many Owls Valley (Nose Hill), NW

Hike 8: Bowmont Park West, NW
Hike 9: Bowmont Park East, NW
Hike 10: Bowness Park/Bow River, NW
Hike 12: Confederations Park/Nose Hill, NW
Hike 18: Edworthy Park, SW
Hike 19: Douglas Fir Trail, SW
Hike 23: Inglewood Bird Sanctuary, SE
Hike 30: Beaverdam Flats Park/Carburn Park, SE
Hike 31: Weaselhead Flats/North Glenmore Park, SW
Hike 33: Jackrabbit Trail, SW
Hike 34: Ridgeview Trail (Fish Creek), SW
Hike 35: Raven Rocks (Fish Creek), SW
Hike 36: Bow Valley Ranch (Fish Creek), SE
Hike 37: Mallard Point (Fish Creek), SE

Christmas Lights Hikes

Hike 14: McHugh Bluff/Prince's Island, NW
Hike 15: Regal Terrace/Sunnyside, NE/NW
Hike 20: Bow River/Scarboro, SW
Hike 21: Elbow Park/Mount Royal, SW
Hike 22: Ramsay/Inglewood, SE
Hike 24: Roxboro/Stanley Park, SW
Hike 29: Britannia/Parkhill, SW

Winter Wonderland Evening Walks

Hike 13: Briar Hill/Parkdale, NW
Hike 15: Regal Terrace/Sunnyside, NE/NW
Hike 16: Bridgeland/Bow River, NE
Hike 21: Elbow Park/Mount Royal, SW
Hike 22: Ramsay/Inglewood, SE
Hike 26: Garrison Woods/Marda Loop, SW

Winter Wonderland Daylight Hikes

Hike 8: Bowmont Park West, NW (bring poles)
Hike 9: Bowmont Park East, NW (bring poles)
Hike 12: Confederation Park/Nose Hill, NW
Hike 23: Inglewood Bird Sanctuary, SE
Hike 25: Reader Rock Garden/Elbow River, SW
Hike 27: Glenmore Dam/Bel-Aire, SW
Hike 28: Sandy Beach/Mount Royal, SW

Hike 31: Weaselhead Flats/North Glenmore Park, SW
Hike 34: Ridgeview Trail (Fish Creek), SW
Hike 35: Raven Rocks (Fish Creek), SW
Hike 36: Bow Valley Ranch (Fish Creek), SE
Hike 37: Mallard Point (Fish Creek), SE

Summer Home-and-Garden Hikes

Hike 15: Regal Terrace/Sunnyside, NE/NW
Hike 21: Elbow Park/Mount Royal, SW
Hike 24: Roxboro/Stanley Park, SW
Hike 25: Reader Rock Garden/Elbow River, SW
Hike 28: Sandy Beach/Mount Royal, SW
Hike 29: Britannia/Parkhill, SW

Fall Colour Hikes

Hike 1: Twelve Mile Coulee, NW
Hike 5: Porcupine Valley (Nose Hill), NW
Hike 6: Rubbing Stone Hill (Nose Hill), NW
Hike 7: Many Owls Valley (Nose Hill), NW
Hike 8: Bowmont Park West, NW
Hike 9: Bowmont Park East, NW
Hike 19: Douglas Fir Trail, SW
Hike 23: Inglewood Bird Sanctuary, SE
Hike 27: Glenmore Dam/Bel-Aire, SW
Hike 28: Sandy Beach/Mount Royal, SW
Hike 30: Beaverdam Flats Park/Carburn Park, SE
Hike 31: Weaselhead Flats/North Glenmore Park, SW
Hike 33: Jackrabbit Trail, SW
Hike 34: Ridgeview Trail (Fish Creek), SW
Hike 35: Raven Rocks (Fish Creek), SW
Hike 36: Bow Valley Ranch (Fish Creek), SE
Hike 37: Mallard Point (Fish Creek), SE

Dogs' Favourite Hikes (with off-leash areas)

Hike 1: Twelve Mile Coulee, NW
Hike 6: Rubbing Stone Hill (Nose Hill), NW
Hike 8: Bowmont Park West, NW
Hike 9: Bowmont Park East, NW
Hike 18: Edworthy Park, SW

Hike 27: Glenmore Dam/Bel-Aire, SW
Hike 28: Sandy Beach/Mount Royal, SW

Historic Neighbourhood Hikes

Hike 16: Bridgeland/Bow River, NE
Hike 21: Elbow Park/Mount Royal, SW
Hike 22: Ramsay/Inglewood, SE

Index

(the numbers listed in parentheses are the hike numbers)

Aerobic exercise 3
Altadore (26,27)
Anaerobic exercise 3
Annie's Café (36 a & b)
Backpacks 17
Bagelmakers (14)
Bankside (Fish Creek Park) (37)
Bankview (20)
Beaverdam Flats (30)
Beavers (36 a & b)
Bebo Grove (Fish Creek Park) (35)
Bel-Aire (27)
Bell's Bookstore Café (26, 28)
Birds (23, 35)
Boots 16
Bow Valley Ranch (Fish Creek Park) (36a & b)
Bowmont Natural Environment Park (9, 10)
Bowness (12)
Bowness Park (8)
Briar Hill (13)
Brickburn (19)
Bridgeland (16)
Britannia (29)
Burnsmead (Fish Creek Park) (37)
Calgary overview map ix
Carburn Park (30)
Chinatown (16)
Clothing, hiking 14–16
Confederation Park (11)
Coyotes (28)
Crescent Heights (14, 15)
Currie (26)
Deer (34)
Douglas Fir Trail (19)
Eau Claire Market (14)
Edgemont Hikes (2, 3)
Edworthy Park (18, 19)
Elbow Park (21,24,26,28)

Elboya (29)
Elevation 38
Fish Creek Park Hikes (24,35,36 a&b, 37)
Food 13–14
Footwear 16
Garrison Woods (26)
Gear, hiking 14–18
Glengarry (20)
Glenmore Reservoir Hikes (27, 31, 32, 33)
Good Earth Café (33)
Heart Rate 4–6
Heartland Café (14)
Hills 5, 6, 16, 17, 21
Hull's Wood (Fish Creek Park) (36 a & b)
Inglewood (22)
Inglewood Bird Sanctuary (23)
Jackrabbit Trail (33)
Java Temptations (8)
Kaffa Café and Salsa House (26, 28)
Knob Hill (20)
Lakeview (32)
Layers, clothing 14–15
Lazy Loaf and Kettle Café (19)
Lina's Italian Market and Cappuccino Bar (15)
Lowery Gardens (19)
Mallard Point (Fish Creek Park) (37)
Manuel Latruwe Belgian Patisserie & Bread Shop (25)
Marda Loop (26)
Mayfair (27)
McHugh Bluff (14)
Montgomery (12)
Mount Royal (21, 24,25, 26)
North Glenmore Park (27, 32)
Nose Hill Hikes (overview, 5, 6, 7)
Park Hill (24, 25)
Parkdale (13)
Parkland (36 a & b)
Pemmican 86
Poles, hiking 17–18
Primal Grounds Café (31, 32)
Princes Island (14)
Ramsay (22)
Raven Rocks (Fish Creek Park) (35)
Reader Rock Garden (25)
Regal Terrace (15)
Renfrew (16)

Rideau Park (29)
Ridegview Trail (Fish Creek Park) (34)
Riley Park (14)
River Park (27, 28)
Riverdale (28, 29)
Riverside (16)
Rosedale (15)
Roxboro (24)
Sandy Beach (28)
Scarboro (20)
Scotsmans Hill (22)
Shannon Terrace (Fish Creek Park) (34)
Shoes 16
Shouldice Park (12)
Sikome Lake (36 a & b)
Silver Springs Area (9, 10)
Socks 16
South Calgary (26)
South Glenmore Park (33)
Stairs (see: hills)
Stanley Park (17, 24)
Strathcona ravine (17)
Stretching exercises 7 (6–10, 12)
Sunalta (20)
Sunnyside (14, 15)
Sunterra Market Café (17)
Tom Campbells Hill (16)
Tuscany (1)
Twelve Mile Coulee (1)
Union Cemetery (25)
Valley Ridge (8)
Walker, James (23)
Warm-up 6–10
Weaselhead Flats (31)
West Hillhurst (13)
West Nose Creek Park (4)
Wildwood (18)